SIMPLY DELICIOUS DESSERTS

with Eagle® Brand Sweetened Condensed Milk

IF IT'S BORDEN-IT'S GOT TO BE GOOD

Dessert—it's our favorite word! Americans love dessert all year round. From cool summertime Creamy Lemon Pie to festive holiday Foolproof Dark Chocolate Fudge, Eagle® Brand Sweetened Condensed Milk recipes are traditional favorites in many families.

Eagle Brand is the dessert maker consumers have trusted for more than 130 years for its wholesome goodness and consistent high quality. All-natural Eagle Brand makes it easy to create delicious desserts that are irresistible. No-bake pie fillings, rich chocolate sauces, and creamy smooth ice creams are all simply made in just moments with Eagle Brand magic.

Our newest collection of SIMPLY DELICIOUS DESSERTS is brimming with wonderful ideas from the Borden Kitchens. Once you've tried a few recipes, you'll see why we say that every dessert made with Eagle® Brand Sweetened Condensed Milk is "Easy to make . . . Hard to resist!"™

CREDITS

Borden Kitchens: Annie Watts Cloncs, Director

Charlene Sneed, Senior Home Economist

Design and Production: Mallard Marketing Associates, Inc.

All recipes developed and tested by the home economists of the Borden Kitchens.

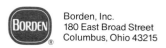 Borden, Inc.
180 East Broad Street
Columbus, Ohio 43215

CONTENTS

Pictured on the cover:
Strawberry Cheese Pie,
Petite Macaroon Cups,
Streusel Caramel Bars,
Fudge Nut Brownies,
Fudge Ribbon Cake

SIMPLY DELICIOUS
DESSERTS

with Eagle® Brand Sweetened Condensed Milk

NEW MAGIC
in the kitchen

Try a
Touch

ORDEN'S

CLA
DESS
FROM THE D
EAGLE® BRAND SWEE

VO
MAGIC

SIMPLY DELIC
DESSERTS
with Eagle® Brand Sweetened Conc

INTRODUCTION

Simply...
At Borden, we understand the importance of convenience in today's busy lifestyle. With that in mind, our kitchens have developed SIMPLY DELICIOUS DESSERTS. You will find our recipes easy, convenient and quick to prepare.

Delicious...
All of the recipes in this cookbook are made with the same premium quality Eagle® Brand Sweetened Condensed Milk that has been a key ingredient in delicious pies, cookies and ice creams for generations. SIMPLY DELICIOUS DESSERTS combines the all-time favorites of the past with new and exciting recipes for your family's enjoyment.

Desserts...
SIMPLY DELICIOUS DESSERTS features more than 150 recipes from Traditional Pumpkin Pie and Magic Cookie Bars to our new Fudge Truffle Cheesecake and Strawberry Brownie Torte. We think you'll agree our newest collection of recipes will give you delicious dessert ideas for any occasion.

PIES

Pictured: Mocha Walnut Tart
(recipe page 8), Peach Amaretto
Cheese Pie (recipe page 9).

MICROWAVE CARAMEL NUT CREAM PIE

(Makes 1 pie)

1 (14-ounce) can Eagle® Brand Sweetened Condensed Milk (NOT evaporated milk)
1 cup chopped nuts
2 tablespoons Borden® Milk
½ teaspoon ground cinnamon
1 cup (½ pint) Borden® Whipping Cream, whipped
1 (6-ounce) packaged graham cracker crumb pie crust

Pour sweetened condensed milk into 2-quart glass measure; cook on 50% power (medium) 4 minutes, stirring briskly every 2 minutes until smooth. Cook on 30% power (medium-low) 12 to 18 minutes or until very thick and caramel-colored, stirring briskly every 2 minutes until smooth. Stir nuts, milk and cinnamon into *warm* caramelized sweetened condensed milk; cool to room temperature. Fold in whipped cream. Pour into crust. Chill 3 hours or until set. Garnish as desired. Refrigerate leftovers.

MOCHA WALNUT TART

(Makes one 9-inch pie)

1 (9-inch) unbaked pastry shell
2 (1-ounce) squares unsweetened chocolate
¼ cup margarine or butter
1 (14-ounce) can Eagle® Brand Sweetened Condensed Milk (NOT evaporated milk)
¼ cup water
2 eggs, well beaten
¼ cup coffee-flavored liqueur
1 teaspoon vanilla extract
⅛ teaspoon salt
1 cup walnuts, toasted and chopped

Preheat oven to 350°. In medium saucepan, over low heat, melt chocolate and margarine. Stir in sweetened condensed milk, water and eggs; *mix well*. Remove from heat; stir in remaining ingredients except walnuts and pastry shell. Pour into pastry shell; top with walnuts. Bake 40 to 45 minutes or until center is set. Cool. Serve warm or chilled. Garnish as desired. Refrigerate leftovers.

Microwave Caramel Nut Cream Pie

MICROWAVE ORANGE CREAM PIE ▲

(Makes one 9-inch pie)

1½ cups gingersnap cookie crumbs (about 28 cookies)
6 tablespoons margarine or butter, melted
1 (14-ounce) can Eagle® Brand Sweetened Condensed Milk (NOT evaporated milk)
¼ cup frozen orange juice concentrate, thawed
2 egg yolks
2 teaspoons grated orange rind
1 (8-ounce) container Borden® Sour Cream, at room temperature
Whipped topping

Combine crumbs and margarine; press firmly on bottom and up side to rim of microwaveable pie plate. Cook on 100% power (high) 2 minutes, rotating plate after 1 minute. Cool. Meanwhile, in 2-quart glass measure, mix sweetened condensed milk, juice concentrate, egg yolks and rind; cook on 100% power (high) 3 to 4 minutes, stirring after 2 minutes. Cool 10 minutes; stir in sour cream. Pour into prepared crust. Chill 3 hours or until set. Spread with whipped topping; garnish as desired. Refrigerate leftovers.

PEACH AMARETTO CHEESE PIE

(Makes one 9-inch pie)

1 (9-inch) unbaked pastry shell
1 (8-ounce) package cream cheese, softened
1 (14-ounce) can Eagle® Brand Sweetened Condensed Milk (NOT evaporated milk)
2 eggs
3 tablespoons amaretto liqueur
1½ teaspoons almond extract
3 medium peaches, peeled, seeded and sliced, or 1 (16-ounce) package frozen peach slices, thawed and well drained
2 tablespoons peach preserves

Preheat oven to 375°. Bake pastry shell 15 minutes. Meanwhile, in large mixer bowl, beat cheese until fluffy. Gradually beat in sweetened condensed milk until smooth. Add eggs, 2 tablespoons amaretto and 1 teaspoon extract; mix well. Pour into prepared pastry shell. Bake 25 minutes or until set. Cool. Arrange peach slices on top of pie. In small saucepan, combine preserves, remaining 1 tablespoon amaretto and remaining ½ teaspoon extract; over low heat, cook and stir until hot. Spoon over top of pie. Chill. Garnish as desired. Refrigerate leftovers.

PEPPERMINT PARFAIT PIE

(Makes one 9-inch pie)

- 1 (9-inch) baked pastry shell
- 1 (1-ounce) square unsweetened chocolate
- 1 (14-ounce) can Eagle® Brand Sweetened Condensed Milk (NOT evaporated milk)
- ½ teaspoon vanilla extract
- 1 (8-ounce) package cream cheese, softened
- 3 tablespoons white creme de menthe Red food coloring, optional
- 1 (8-ounce) container frozen non-dairy whipped topping, thawed (3½ cups)

In small saucepan, melt chocolate with ½ cup sweetened condensed milk; stir in vanilla. Spread on bottom of prepared pastry shell. In large mixer bowl, beat cheese until fluffy. Gradually beat in remaining sweetened condensed milk. Stir in creme de menthe and food coloring if desired. Fold in whipped topping. Pour into prepared pastry shell. Chill 4 hours or until set. Garnish as desired. Refrigerate leftovers.

FLUFFY GRASSHOPPER PIE

(Makes one 9-inch pie)

- 2 cups finely crushed creme-filled chocolate sandwich cookies (about 20 cookies)
- ¼ cup margarine or butter, melted
- 1 (8-ounce) package cream cheese, softened
- 1 (14-ounce) can Eagle® Brand Sweetened Condensed Milk (NOT evaporated milk)
- 3 tablespoons ReaLemon® Lemon Juice from Concentrate
- ¼ cup green creme de menthe
- ¼ cup white creme de cacao
- 1 (4-ounce) container frozen non-dairy whipped topping, thawed (1¾ cups)

Combine crumbs and margarine; press firmly on bottom and up side to rim of buttered 9-inch pie plate. Chill. Meanwhile, in large mixer bowl, beat cheese until fluffy. Gradually beat in sweetened condensed milk until smooth. Stir in ReaLemon® brand and liqueurs. Fold in whipped topping. Chill 20 minutes; pour into crust. Chill or freeze 4 hours or until set. Garnish as desired. Refrigerate or freeze leftovers.

Peppermint Parfait Pie, Fluffy Grasshopper Pie

FUDGE DELUXE PIE ▲

(Makes one 9-inch pie)

1 (9-inch) baked pastry shell
3 (1-ounce) squares unsweetened or
   semi-sweet chocolate
1 (14-ounce) can Eagle® Brand
   Sweetened Condensed Milk
   (NOT evaporated milk)
¼ teaspoon salt
¼ cup hot water
2 egg yolks
1 teaspoon vanilla extract
1 cup (½ pint) Borden® Whipping
   Cream
   Additional whipped cream

In heavy saucepan, over medium heat, melt chocolate with sweetened condensed milk and salt. Cook and stir rapidly until *very thick* and bubbly, 5 to 8 minutes. Add water and egg yolks; cook and stir rapidly until mixture thickens and bubbles again. Remove from heat; stir in vanilla. Cool 15 minutes. *Chill thoroughly*, about 30 minutes; stir. In large mixer bowl, beat *1 cup* whipping cream until stiff; fold into cooled chocolate mixture. Pour into prepared pastry shell. Chill 3 hours or until set. Spread top with additional whipped cream; garnish as desired. Refrigerate leftovers.

FUDGE BROWNIE PIE ▲

(Makes one 9-inch pie)

1 (9-inch) unbaked pastry shell
1 (6-ounce) package semi-sweet
   chocolate chips (1 cup)
¼ cup margarine or butter
1 (14-ounce) can Eagle® Brand
   Sweetened Condensed Milk
   (NOT evaporated milk)
½ cup biscuit baking mix
2 eggs
1 teaspoon vanilla extract
1 cup chopped nuts

Preheat oven to 375°. Bake pastry shell 10 minutes; remove from oven. Reduce oven temperature to 325°. In saucepan, over low heat, melt chips with margarine. In large mixer bowl, beat chocolate mixture with remaining ingredients except nuts until smooth. Add nuts. Pour into prepared pastry shell. Bake 35 to 40 minutes or until center is set. Cool slightly. Serve with ice cream if desired. Refrigerate leftovers.

11

FLUFFY YOGURT FRUIT PIE ▲

(Makes one 9-inch pie)

1 (9-inch) graham cracker crumb crust
   or baked pastry shell
1 (8-ounce) package cream cheese,
   softened
1 (14-ounce) can Eagle® Brand
   Sweetened Condensed Milk
   (NOT evaporated milk)
1 (8-ounce) container Borden®
   Lite-line® Strawberry or other
   fruit Yogurt
2 tablespoons ReaLemon® Lemon
   Juice from Concentrate
   Red or other food coloring,
   optional
1 (8-ounce) container frozen
   non-dairy whipped topping,
   thawed (3½ cups)
   Strawberries or other fresh fruit

In large mixer bowl, beat cheese until
fluffy. Gradually beat in sweetened condensed milk until smooth. Stir in yogurt,
ReaLemon® brand and food coloring if
desired. Fold in whipped topping. Pour
into prepared crust. Chill 4 hours or until
set. Garnish with strawberries. Refrigerate
leftovers.

LEMON KIWIFRUIT PIE ▲

(Makes one 9-inch pie)

1 (9-inch) baked pastry shell
1 (14-ounce) can Eagle® Brand
   Sweetened Condensed Milk
   (NOT evaporated milk)
1 (6-ounce) can frozen lemonade or
   limeade concentrate, thawed
   Yellow food coloring, optional
1 (8-ounce) container frozen
   non-dairy whipped topping,
   thawed (3½ cups)
2 kiwifruits, peeled and sliced

In large bowl, combine sweetened condensed milk, lemonade concentrate and
food coloring if desired; mix well. Fold in
whipped topping. Pour into prepared pastry
shell. Chill 4 hours or until set. Garnish
with kiwifruit. Refrigerate leftovers.

CHOCOLATE TRUFFLE PIE ▲

(Makes one 9- or 10-inch pie)

1 (9- or 10-inch) chocolate crumb crust
1 envelope unflavored gelatine
½ cup water
3 (1-ounce) squares unsweetened or semi-sweet chocolate, melted and cooled
1 (14-ounce) can Eagle® Brand Sweetened Condensed Milk (NOT evaporated milk)
1 teaspoon vanilla extract
2 cups (1 pint) Borden® Whipping Cream, whipped

In small saucepan, sprinkle gelatine over water; let stand 1 minute. Over low heat, stir until gelatine dissolves. Cool. In large mixer bowl, beat chocolate with sweetened condensed milk until smooth. Stir in gelatine mixture and vanilla. Fold in whipped cream. Pour into prepared crust. Chill 3 hours or until set. Garnish as desired. Refrigerate leftovers.

FROZEN ORANGE CLOUD PIE ▲

(Makes one 9-inch pie)

2 cups vanilla wafer crumbs (about 50 wafers)
⅓ cup margarine or butter, melted
1 (14-ounce) can Eagle® Brand Sweetened Condensed Milk (NOT evaporated milk)
½ cup orange carbonated beverage
2 to 3 teaspoons grated orange rind Red and yellow food coloring, optional
2 cups (1 pint) Borden® Whipping Cream, stiffly whipped

Combine crumbs and margarine; press firmly on bottom and up side to rim of 9-inch pie plate. In large bowl, combine sweetened condensed milk, carbonated beverage, rind and food coloring if desired; mix well. Fold in whipped cream. Pour into prepared crust. Freeze 6 hours or until firm. Let stand 10 minutes before serving. Garnish as desired. Freeze leftovers.

FROZEN CRANBERRY CHEESE PIE

(Makes one 9-inch pie)

- 1½ cups vanilla wafer crumbs (about 40 wafers)
- 6 tablespoons margarine or butter, melted
- 2 (3-ounce) packages cream cheese, softened
- 1 (14-ounce) can Eagle® Brand Sweetened Condensed Milk (NOT evaporated milk)
- ⅓ cup ReaLemon® Lemon Juice from Concentrate
- 1 teaspoon vanilla extract
  Red food coloring, optional
- 1 (16-ounce) can whole berry cranberry sauce
  Whipped cream

Combine crumbs and margarine; press firmly on bottom and up side to rim of 9-inch pie plate. Chill. Meanwhile, in large mixer bowl, beat cheese until fluffy. Gradually beat in sweetened condensed milk until smooth. Stir in ReaLemon® brand, vanilla and food coloring if desired. Reserving ½ cup cranberry sauce, add remainder to cheese mixture. Pour into prepared crust. Cover; freeze 6 hours or until firm. Just before serving, garnish with whipped cream and reserved cranberry sauce. Freeze leftovers.

LEMON ANGEL PIE ▶

(Makes one 9-inch pie)

Meringue Crust
- 1 (14-ounce) can Eagle® Brand Sweetened Condensed Milk (NOT evaporated milk)
- ⅓ cup ReaLemon® Lemon Juice from Concentrate
- 2 teaspoons grated lemon rind
  Yellow food coloring, optional
- 3 egg whites*
- ¼ teaspoon cream of tartar
- 1 cup (½ pint) Borden® Whipping Cream, whipped

Prepare Meringue Crust. In large bowl, combine sweetened condensed milk, ReaLemon® brand, rind and food coloring if desired; mix well. In small mixer bowl, beat egg whites with cream of tartar until stiff but not dry; gently fold into sweetened condensed milk mixture. Fold in whipped cream. Pour into prepared crust. Chill 3 hours or until set. Garnish as desired. Refrigerate leftovers.

Meringue Crust: Preheat oven to 275°. In small mixer bowl, beat 3 egg whites*, ½ teaspoon vanilla extract and ¼ teaspoon cream of tartar until soft peaks form. Gradually add ½ cup sugar, beating until stiff but not dry. Spread on bottom and up side of *well-buttered* 9-inch pie plate to form crust. Bake 1 hour. Turn oven off; leave crust in oven 1 hour. Cool to room temperature.

*Use only Grade A clean, uncracked eggs.

Frozen Cranberry Cheese Pie

ALMOND PUMPKIN PIE

(Makes one 9-inch pie)

1 (9-inch) unbaked pastry shell
1 (16-ounce) can pumpkin (2 cups)
1 (14-ounce) can Eagle® Brand
Sweetened Condensed Milk
(NOT evaporated milk)
2 eggs
1 teaspoon almond extract
½ teaspoon ground cinnamon
1 (6-ounce) package almond brickle
chips, or 1 cup almonds, toasted
and finely chopped

Preheat oven to 425°. In large mixer bowl, combine all ingredients except pastry shell and brickle chips; mix well. Stir in ½ cup brickle chips. Pour into pastry shell. Top with remaining brickle chips. Bake 15 minutes. Reduce oven temperature to 350°; bake 30 minutes longer or until knife inserted near center comes out clean. Cool. Garnish as desired. Refrigerate leftovers.

Almond Pumpkin Pie

CHOCOLATE AMARETTO PIE ▲

(Makes one 9-inch pie)

1   (9-inch) unbaked pastry shell
1   (3-ounce) package cream
    cheese, softened
2   (1-ounce) squares unsweetened
    chocolate, melted
⅛   teaspoon salt
1   (14-ounce) can Eagle® Brand
    Sweetened Condensed Milk
    (NOT evaporated milk)
2   eggs
¼   to ⅓ cup amaretto liqueur
1   cup sliced or chopped almonds,
    toasted if desired

Preheat oven to 350°. In large mixer bowl,
beat cheese, chocolate and salt until well
blended. Gradually beat in sweetened
condensed milk until smooth. Add eggs;
mix well. Stir in liqueur and almonds.
Pour into pastry shell. Bake 30 to 35 minutes or until center is set. Cool. Serve
warm or chilled. Garnish as desired.
Refrigerate leftovers.

DEEP-DISH PUMPKIN PIE ▲

(Makes 8 to 10 servings)

1¾ cups unsifted flour
⅓   cup firmly packed brown sugar
⅓   cup granulated sugar
1   cup cold margarine or butter,
    cut into small pieces
1   cup chopped nuts
1   (16-ounce) can pumpkin (2 cups)
1   (14-ounce) can Eagle® Brand
    Sweetened Condensed Milk
    (NOT evaporated milk)
2   eggs
1   teaspoon ground cinnamon
½   teaspoon ground allspice
½   teaspoon salt

Preheat oven to 350°. In medium bowl,
combine flour and sugars; cut in margarine until crumbly. Stir in nuts. Reserving
1 cup crumb mixture, press remainder
firmly on bottom and halfway up sides of
12x7-inch baking dish. In large mixer bowl,
combine remaining ingredients except
reserved crumb mixture; mix well. Pour
into prepared dish. Top with reserved
crumb mixture. Bake 55 minutes or until
golden. Cool. Serve with ice cream if
desired. Refrigerate leftovers.

PEANUT BUTTER PIE

(Makes one 9-inch pie)

- 1 (9-inch) baked pastry shell
- ⅓ cup peanut butter
- ¾ cup confectioners' sugar
- 1 (14-ounce) can Eagle® Brand Sweetened Condensed Milk (NOT evaporated milk)
- 4 eggs*, separated
- ½ cup water
- 1 (4-serving size) package vanilla flavor pudding mix *(not instant)*
- 1 (8-ounce) container Borden® Sour Cream, at room temperature
- ¼ teaspoon cream of tartar
- 6 tablespoons granulated sugar

In small bowl, cut peanut butter into confectioners' sugar until crumbly; sprinkle into pastry shell. In large saucepan, mix sweetened condensed milk, egg yolks, water and pudding mix; cook and stir until thickened. Cool slightly; stir in sour cream. Spoon into prepared pastry shell. In small mixer bowl, beat egg whites with cream of tartar to soft peaks; gradually beat in granulated sugar until stiff. Spread on pie, sealing carefully to edge of shell. Bake in preheated 350° oven 15 minutes or until golden. Cool. Chill. Refrigerate leftovers.

MICROWAVE: Prepare peanut butter and confectioners' sugar as above. In 2-quart glass measure, mix sweetened condensed milk, egg yolks, water and pudding mix; cook on 100% power (high) 6 to 8 minutes, stirring after 3 minutes then every minute until thickened. Proceed as above.

*Use only Grade A clean, uncracked eggs.

COCONUT CUSTARD PIE

(Makes one 9-inch pie)

- 1 (9-inch) unbaked pastry shell
- 1 cup flaked coconut
- 3 eggs
- 1 (14-ounce) can Eagle® Brand Sweetened Condensed Milk (NOT evaporated milk)
- 1¼ cups hot water
- 1 teaspoon vanilla extract
- ¼ teaspoon salt
- ⅛ teaspoon ground nutmeg

Preheat oven to 425°. Toast ½ cup coconut; set aside. Bake pastry shell 8 minutes; cool slightly. Meanwhile, in medium bowl, beat eggs. Add sweetened condensed milk, water, vanilla, salt and nutmeg; mix well. Stir in remaining ½ cup coconut. Pour into pastry shell. Sprinkle with toasted coconut. Bake 10 minutes. Reduce oven temperature to 350°; bake 25 to 30 minutes longer or until knife inserted near center comes out clean. Cool. Chill if desired. Refrigerate leftovers.

Custard Pie: Omit coconut. Proceed as above.

Coconut Custard Pie, Peanut Butter Pie

QUICK BUTTERSCOTCH CHEESE PIE

(Makes one 9-inch pie)

- 1 (9-inch) baked pastry shell or graham cracker crumb crust
- 1 (8-ounce) package cream cheese, softened
- 1 (14-ounce) can Eagle® Brand Sweetened Condensed Milk (NOT evaporated milk)
- ¾ cup cold water
- 1 (4-serving size) package *instant* butterscotch flavor pudding mix
- 1 cup (½ pint) Borden® Whipping Cream, whipped

In large mixer bowl, beat cheese until fluffy; gradually beat in sweetened condensed milk until smooth. On low speed, beat in water and pudding mix until smooth. Fold in whipped cream. Pour into prepared pastry shell. Chill 2 hours or until set. Garnish as desired. Refrigerate leftovers.

Chocolate Cheese Pie: Substitute *instant* chocolate flavor pudding mix for butterscotch. Add ¼ cup unsweetened cocoa with pudding mix. Proceed as above.

Coconut Cheese Pie: Substitute *instant* coconut cream flavor pudding mix for butterscotch. Fold in ½ cup flaked coconut with whipped cream. Proceed as above.

Vanilla Nut Cheese Pie: Substitute *instant* vanilla flavor pudding mix for butterscotch. Fold in ¾ cup chopped toasted nuts with whipped cream. Proceed as above.

LEMON SPONGE PIE

(Makes one 9-inch pie)

- 1 (9-inch) unbaked pastry shell
- 3 eggs, separated
- 1 (14-ounce) can Eagle® Brand Sweetened Condensed Milk (NOT evaporated milk)
- ⅓ cup ReaLemon® Lemon Juice from Concentrate
- 2 tablespoons flour
- 2 teaspoons grated lemon rind Yellow food coloring, optional

Pictured from top: Quick Butterscotch Cheese Pie, Lemon Sponge Pie.

Preheat oven to 375°. Bake pastry shell 10 minutes; remove from oven. Reduce oven temperature to 350°. In large mixer bowl, combine remaining ingredients except egg whites; mix well. In small mixer bowl, beat egg whites until stiff but not dry; fold into lemon mixture. Pour into prepared pastry shell. Bake 25 minutes or until set. Cool. Serve warm or chilled. Garnish as desired. Refrigerate leftovers.

SPIRITED CHOCOLATE CREAM TARTS

(Makes 10 to 12 tarts)

- 1 **(14-ounce) can Eagle® Brand Sweetened Condensed Milk (NOT evaporated milk)**
- 2 **tablespoons orange-, almond- or coffee-flavored liqueur or brandy**
- 2 **tablespoons cold water**
- 1 **(4-serving size) package** *instant* **chocolate flavor pudding mix**
- ¼ **cup unsweetened cocoa**
- 1 **cup (½ pint) Borden® Whipping Cream, whipped**
- 10 **to 12 (3-inch) prepared tart-size crusts**

In large mixer bowl, beat sweetened condensed milk, liqueur and water until well blended; add pudding mix and cocoa. Beat until smooth. Chill 5 minutes. Fold in whipped cream. Spoon equal portions into crusts. Chill. Garnish as desired. Refrigerate leftovers.

Spirited Chocolate Cream Tarts

TRADITIONAL PUMPKIN PIE

(Makes one 9-inch pie)

- 1 (9-inch) unbaked pastry shell
- 1 (16-ounce) can pumpkin (2 cups)
- 1 (14-ounce) can Eagle® Brand Sweetened Condensed Milk (NOT evaporated milk)
- 2 eggs
- 1 teaspoon ground cinnamon
- ½ teaspoon ground ginger
- ½ teaspoon ground nutmeg
- ½ teaspoon salt

Preheat oven to 425°. In large mixer bowl, combine all ingredients except pastry shell; mix well. Pour into pastry shell. Bake 15 minutes. Reduce oven temperature to 350°; bake 35 to 40 minutes longer or until knife inserted 1 inch from edge comes out clean. Cool. Garnish as desired. Refrigerate leftovers.

Sour Cream Topping: In medium bowl, combine 1½ cups Borden® Sour Cream, 2 tablespoons sugar and 1 teaspoon vanilla extract. After 30 minutes of baking, spread evenly over top of pie; bake 10 minutes longer. Garnish as desired.

Streusel Topping: In medium bowl, combine ½ cup firmly packed light brown sugar and ½ cup unsifted flour; cut in ¼ cup cold margarine or butter until crumbly. Stir in ¼ cup chopped nuts. After 30 minutes of baking, sprinkle on top of pie; bake 10 minutes longer.

ORANGE BLOSSOM PIE

(Makes one 9-inch pie)

- 1 (9-inch) unbaked pastry shell
- 1 (14-ounce) can Eagle® Brand Sweetened Condensed Milk (NOT evaporated milk)
- 1 cup orange juice
- 2 egg yolks
- 1 tablespoon grated orange rind
- 1 (3-ounce) package cream cheese, softened
- ½ cup Borden® Sour Cream, at room temperature
- ½ cup confectioners' sugar
- ½ teaspoon vanilla extract

Preheat oven to 375°. Bake pastry shell 15 minutes. Remove from oven; reduce oven temperature to 325°. In large bowl, combine sweetened condensed milk, orange juice, egg yolks and rind; mix well. Pour into prepared pastry shell (mixture will be thin). Bake 35 minutes or until set. Meanwhile, in small mixer bowl, beat remaining ingredients until smooth. Spread over pie. Bake 5 minutes longer. Cool. Chill. Garnish as desired. Refrigerate leftovers.

Pictured from top: Orange Blossom Pie, Traditional Pumpkin Pie.

CREAMY LEMON PIE ▲

(Makes one 8- or 9-inch pie)

1 (8- or 9-inch) baked pastry shell or
   graham cracker crumb crust
3 egg yolks*
1 (14-ounce) can Eagle® Brand
   Sweetened Condensed Milk
   (NOT evaporated milk)
½ cup ReaLemon® Lemon Juice
   from Concentrate
   Yellow food coloring, optional
   Whipped topping or whipped cream

Preheat oven to 325°. In medium bowl,
beat egg yolks; stir in sweetened condensed milk, ReaLemon® brand and
food coloring if desired. Pour into prepared pastry shell; bake 30 minutes. Cool.
Chill. Spread with whipped topping. Garnish as desired. Refrigerate leftovers.

*Use only Grade A clean, uncracked eggs.

CHERRY CHEESE PIE ▲

(Makes one 9-inch pie)

1 (9-inch) graham cracker crumb
   crust or baked pastry shell
1 (8-ounce) package cream cheese,
   softened
1 (14-ounce) can Eagle® Brand
   Sweetened Condensed Milk
   (NOT evaporated milk)
⅓ cup ReaLemon® Lemon Juice
   from Concentrate
1 teaspoon vanilla extract
1 (21-ounce) can cherry pie filling,
   chilled

In large mixer bowl, beat cheese until
fluffy. Gradually beat in sweetened
condensed milk until smooth. Stir in
ReaLemon® brand and vanilla. Pour into
prepared crust. Chill 3 hours or until set.
Top with desired amount of pie filling
before serving. Refrigerate leftovers.

Banana Cream Cheese Pie: Omit cherry
pie filling. Prepare cheese mixture as
above. Slice 2 bananas; dip in ReaLemon®
brand, drain and line crust. Pour filling over
bananas; cover. Chill. Before serving, slice
2 bananas; dip in ReaLemon® brand,
drain and garnish top of pie.

STRAWBERRY CHEESE PIE

(Makes one 9-inch pie)

1 (9-inch) baked pastry shell or
   graham cracker crumb crust
1 (8-ounce) package cream cheese,
   softened
1 (14-ounce) can Eagle® Brand
   Sweetened Condensed Milk
   (NOT evaporated milk)
⅓ cup ReaLemon® Lemon Juice
   from Concentrate
1 teaspoon vanilla extract
1 quart fresh strawberries, cleaned
   and hulled
1 (16-ounce) package prepared
   strawberry glaze, chilled

In large mixer bowl, beat cheese until
fluffy. Gradually beat in sweetened
condensed milk until smooth. Stir in
ReaLemon® brand and vanilla. Pour
into prepared pastry shell. Chill 3 hours
or until set. Top with strawberries and
desired amount of glaze. Refrigerate
leftovers.

22

KEY LIME PIE

(Makes one 9- or 10-inch pie)

1 (9- or 10-inch) baked pastry shell or graham cracker crumb crust*
6 egg yolks**
2 (14-ounce) cans Eagle® Brand Sweetened Condensed Milk (NOT evaporated milk)
1 (8-ounce) bottle ReaLime® Lime Juice from Concentrate
Yellow or green food coloring, optional
Whipped cream or whipped topping

Preheat oven to 325°. In large mixer bowl, beat egg yolks with sweetened condensed milk. Stir in ReaLime® brand and food coloring if desired. Pour into prepared pastry shell; bake 40 minutes. Cool. Chill. Top with whipped cream.
Garnish as desired.
Refrigerate leftovers.

*If using frozen packaged pie shell or 6-ounce packaged graham cracker crumb pie crust, use 1 can Eagle® Brand Sweetened Condensed Milk, 3 egg yolks and ½ cup ReaLime® brand. Bake 30 minutes. Proceed as above.

**Use only Grade A clean, uncracked eggs.

BLUEBERRY STREUSEL COBBLER ▲

(Makes 8 to 12 servings)

1   **pint fresh or frozen blueberries**
1   **(14-ounce) can Eagle® Brand Sweetened Condensed Milk (NOT evaporated milk)**
2   **teaspoons grated lemon rind**
¾   **cup plus 2 tablespoons cold margarine or butter**
2   **cups biscuit baking mix**
½   **cup firmly packed brown sugar**
½   **cup chopped nuts**
    Blueberry Sauce

Preheat oven to 325°. In bowl, combine blueberries, sweetened condensed milk and rind. In large bowl, cut ¾ *cup* margarine into *1 ½ cups* biscuit mix until crumbly; add blueberry mixture. Spread in greased 9-inch square baking pan. In small bowl, combine remaining ½ *cup* biscuit mix and sugar; cut in remaining *2 tablespoons* margarine until crumbly. Add nuts. Sprinkle over cobbler. Bake 1 hour and 10 minutes or until golden. Serve warm with vanilla ice cream and Blueberry Sauce. Refrigerate leftovers.

Blueberry Sauce: In saucepan, combine ½ cup sugar, 1 tablespoon cornstarch, ½ teaspoon ground cinnamon and ¼ teaspoon ground nutmeg. Gradually add ½ cup water. Cook and stir until thickened. Stir in 1 pint blueberries; cook and stir until hot. (Makes about 1⅔ cups)

CREATE-A-CRUST APPLE CUSTARD PIE ▲

(Makes one 10-inch pie)

2   **medium all-purpose apples, cored, pared and sliced**
1   **tablespoon ReaLemon® Lemon Juice from Concentrate**
½   **cup plus 2 tablespoons biscuit baking mix**
1   **(14-ounce) can Eagle® Brand Sweetened Condensed Milk (NOT evaporated milk)**
1½   **cups water**
3   **eggs**
¼   **cup margarine or butter, softened**
1½   **teaspoons vanilla extract**
½   **teaspoon ground cinnamon**
½   **teaspoon ground nutmeg**
    Crumb Topping

Preheat oven to 350°. Toss apples with ReaLemon® brand then *2 tablespoons* biscuit mix; arrange in buttered 10-inch pie plate. In blender, combine remaining ingredients except Crumb Topping. Blend on low speed 3 minutes; let stand 5 minutes. Pour over apples; top with Crumb Topping. Bake 35 minutes or until golden. Cool. Garnish as desired. Refrigerate leftovers.

Crumb Topping: In small bowl, combine ½ cup *each* biscuit baking mix and firmly packed brown sugar; cut in ¼ cup cold margarine or butter until crumbly. Add ¼ cup chopped nuts. (Makes about 2 cups)

LIME CREAM PIE

(Makes 1 pie)

1 (14-ounce) can Eagle® Brand
    Sweetened Condensed Milk
    (NOT evaporated milk)
½ cup ReaLime® Lime Juice
    from Concentrate
    Green food coloring, optional
1 cup (½ pint) Borden® Whipping
    Cream, whipped
1 (6-ounce) packaged graham cracker
    crumb pie crust

In medium bowl, stir together sweetened condensed milk, ReaLime® brand and food coloring if desired. Fold in whipped cream. Pour into crust. Chill 3 hours or until set. Garnish as desired. Refrigerate leftovers.

Lemon Cream Pie: Substitute ½ cup ReaLemon® Lemon Juice from Concentrate for ReaLime® brand.

FROZEN CHOCOLATE MOUSSE PIE

(Makes one 9-inch pie)

2 cups finely crushed creme-filled
    chocolate sandwich cookies
    (about 20 cookies)
¼ cup margarine or butter, melted
1 (6-ounce) package semi-sweet
    chocolate chips (1 cup), *or*
    4 (1-ounce) squares semi-
    sweet chocolate, melted
1 (14-ounce) can Eagle® Brand
    Sweetened Condensed Milk
    (NOT evaporated milk)
1½ teaspoons vanilla extract
1 cup (½ pint) Borden® Whipping
    Cream, stiffly whipped

Combine crumbs and margarine; press on bottom and up side to rim of lightly buttered 9-inch pie plate. Chill. In large mixer bowl, beat chocolate with sweetened condensed milk and vanilla until well blended. Chill 10 to 15 minutes. Fold in whipped cream. Pour into prepared crust. Freeze 6 hours or until firm. Garnish as desired. Freeze leftovers.

Lime Cream Pie, Frozen Chocolate Mousse Pie

APPLE CHESS PIE

(Makes one 9-inch pie)

1 (9-inch) unbaked pastry shell
4 eggs
1 (14-ounce) can Eagle® Brand
   Sweetened Condensed Milk
   (NOT evaporated milk)
1 cup applesauce
½ cup margarine or butter, melted
½ cup shredded all-purpose apple
3 tablespoons ReaLemon® Lemon
   Juice from Concentrate
2 tablespoons cornmeal

Preheat oven to 425°. Bake pastry shell 8 minutes; remove from oven. Reduce oven temperature to 350°. In large mixer bowl, beat eggs. Add remaining ingredients except pastry shell; mix well. Pour into prepared pastry shell. Bake 40 minutes or until knife inserted near center comes out clean. Cool. Serve warm or chilled. Garnish as desired. Refrigerate leftovers.

Pineapple Chess Pie: Omit applesauce, shredded apple and ReaLemon® brand. Reduce margarine or butter to ⅓ cup. Add 1 (8-ounce) can juice-packed crushed pineapple, *undrained*, and ½ cup pineapple juice. Proceed as above.

NESSELRODE CREAM PIE ▶

(Makes one 9-inch pie)

   Chocolate Coconut Crust
1 envelope unflavored gelatine
¼ cup water
1 (14-ounce) can Eagle® Brand
   Sweetened Condensed Milk
   (NOT evaporated milk)
¼ cup Borden® Sour Cream
2 tablespoons light rum
½ cup chopped mixed candied fruit
½ cup chopped nuts
¼ cup raisins
2 teaspoons grated orange rind
1 cup (½ pint) Borden® Whipping
   Cream, whipped

Prepare Chocolate Coconut Crust. In small saucepan, sprinkle gelatine over water; let stand 1 minute. Over low heat, stir until gelatine dissolves. In large bowl, combine sweetened condensed milk, sour cream, gelatine mixture and rum. Chill until mixture mounds slightly when dropped from spoon, about 15 minutes. Fold in fruit, nuts, raisins, rind then whipped cream. Pour into prepared crust. Chill 4 hours or until set. Garnish as desired. Refrigerate leftovers.

Chocolate Coconut Crust: In large saucepan, over low heat, melt 2 tablespoons margarine or butter with 1 (1-ounce) square semi-sweet chocolate. Add 1 (7-ounce) package flaked coconut (2⅔ cups); mix well. Press firmly on bottom and up side to rim of buttered 9-inch pie plate. Chill.

Apple Chess Pie

STRAWBERRY DAIQUIRI PIE

(Makes one 9-inch pie)

1 (9-inch) graham cracker crumb
  crust or baked pastry shell
1 (8-ounce) package cream
  cheese, softened
1 (14-ounce) can Eagle® Brand
  Sweetened Condensed Milk
  (NOT evaporated milk)
⅔ cup frozen strawberry daiquiri
  mix, thawed
2 tablespoons light rum
  Red food coloring, optional
1 cup (½ pint) Borden® Whipping
  Cream, whipped
  Fresh strawberries

In large mixer bowl, beat cheese until
fluffy. Gradually beat in sweetened
condensed milk until smooth. Stir in
daiquiri mix, rum and food coloring if
desired. Fold in whipped cream. Pour into
prepared crust. Chill or freeze 4 hours or
until firm. Garnish with strawberries.
Refrigerate or freeze leftovers.

Strawberry Daiquiri Pie

BANANA CREAM PIE

(Makes one 9-inch pie)

- 1 (9-inch) baked pastry shell
- 3 tablespoons cornstarch
- ¼ teaspoon salt
- 1⅔ cups water
- 1 (14-ounce) can Eagle® Brand Sweetened Condensed Milk (NOT evaporated milk)
- 3 egg yolks, beaten
- 2 tablespoons margarine or butter
- 1 teaspoon vanilla extract
- 3 medium bananas
  ReaLemon® Lemon Juice from Concentrate
- 1 cup (½ pint) Borden® Whipping Cream, stiffly whipped

In heavy saucepan, dissolve cornstarch and salt in water; stir in sweetened condensed milk and egg yolks. Cook and stir until thickened and bubbly. Remove from heat; add margarine and vanilla. Cool slightly. Slice *2 bananas;* dip in ReaLemon® brand and drain. Arrange on bottom of prepared pastry shell. Pour filling over bananas; cover. Chill 4 hours or until set. Spread top with whipped cream. Slice remaining banana; dip in ReaLemon® brand, drain and garnish top of pie. Refrigerate leftovers.

SWEET POTATO PECAN PIE

(Makes one 9-inch pie)

- 1 (9-inch) unbaked pastry shell
- 1 pound (2 medium) yams or sweet potatoes, cooked and peeled
- ¼ cup margarine or butter
- 1 (14-ounce) can Eagle® Brand Sweetened Condensed Milk (NOT evaporated milk)
- 1 teaspoon grated orange rind
- 1 teaspoon vanilla extract
- 1 teaspoon ground cinnamon
- ½ teaspoon ground nutmeg
- ¼ teaspoon salt
- 2 eggs
  Pecan Topping

Preheat oven to 350°. In large mixer bowl, beat *hot* yams with margarine until smooth. Add remaining ingredients except pastry shell and Pecan Topping; mix well. Pour into pastry shell. Bake 30 minutes. Remove from oven; spoon Pecan Topping evenly over top. Bake 20 to 25 minutes longer or until golden brown. Cool. Serve warm or chilled. Refrigerate leftovers.

Pecan Topping: In small mixer bowl, combine 1 egg, 3 tablespoons dark corn syrup, 3 tablespoons firmly packed light brown sugar, 1 tablespoon margarine or butter, melted, and ½ teaspoon maple flavoring; mix well. Stir in 1 cup chopped pecans.

Banana Cream Pie, Sweet Potato Pecan Pie

APPLE CUSTARD TART

(Makes one 9- or 10-inch pie)

1 (9- or 10-inch) unbaked pastry
   shell
1½ cups Borden® Sour Cream
1 (14-ounce) can Eagle® Brand
   Sweetened Condensed Milk
   (NOT evaporated milk)
¼ cup frozen apple juice
   concentrate, thawed
1 egg
1½ teaspoons vanilla extract
¼ teaspoon ground cinnamon
2 medium all-purpose apples,
   cored, pared and thinly sliced
1 tablespoon margarine or butter
   Apple Cinnamon Glaze

Preheat oven to 375°. Bake pastry shell
15 minutes. Meanwhile, in small mixer
bowl, beat sour cream, sweetened condensed milk, juice concentrate, egg,
vanilla and cinnamon until smooth. Pour
into prepared pastry shell; bake 30 minutes or until set. Cool. In large skillet,
cook apples in margarine until tender-
crisp. Arrange on top of pie; drizzle with
Apple Cinnamon Glaze. Serve warm or
chilled. Refrigerate leftovers.

Apple Cinnamon Glaze: In small saucepan, combine ¼ cup frozen apple juice
concentrate, thawed, 1 teaspoon cornstarch and ¼ teaspoon ground cinnamon;
mix well. Over low heat, cook and stir
until thickened. (Makes about ¼ cup)

RASPBERRY-TOPPED LEMON PIE ▲

(Makes 1 pie)

1 (10-ounce) package frozen red raspberries in syrup, thawed
1 tablespoon cornstarch
3 egg yolks*
1 (14-ounce) can Eagle® Brand Sweetened Condensed Milk (NOT evaporated milk)
½ cup ReaLemon® Lemon Juice from Concentrate
Yellow food coloring, optional
1 (6-ounce) packaged graham cracker crumb pie crust
Whipped topping

Preheat oven to 325°. In small saucepan, combine raspberries and cornstarch; cook and stir until thickened and clear. In medium bowl, beat egg yolks; stir in sweetened condensed milk, ReaLemon® brand and food coloring if desired. Pour into crust; bake 30 minutes. Spoon raspberry mixture evenly over top. Chill 4 hours or until set. Spread with whipped topping. Garnish as desired. Refrigerate leftovers.

*Use only Grade A clean, uncracked eggs.

BANANA MANDARIN CHEESE PIE ▲

(Makes one 9-inch pie)

1 (9-inch) graham cracker crumb crust
1 (8-ounce) package cream cheese, softened
1 (14-ounce) can Eagle® Brand Sweetened Condensed Milk (NOT evaporated milk)
⅓ cup ReaLemon® Lemon Juice from Concentrate
1 teaspoon vanilla extract
3 medium bananas
Additional ReaLemon® brand
1 (11-ounce) can mandarin orange segments, well drained

In large mixer bowl, beat cheese until fluffy. Gradually beat in sweetened condensed milk until smooth. Stir in ⅓ cup ReaLemon® brand and vanilla. Slice 2 bananas; dip in ReaLemon® brand and drain. Line crust with bananas and about two-thirds of the orange segments. Pour filling over fruit. Chill 3 hours or until set. Before serving, slice remaining banana; dip in ReaLemon® brand and drain. Garnish top with banana slices and remaining orange segments. Refrigerate leftovers.

MINCE VELVET PIE ▲

(Makes one 9-inch pie)

1 (9-inch) unbaked pastry shell
1 (14-ounce) can Eagle® Brand
  Sweetened Condensed Milk
  (NOT evaporated milk)
2 eggs
1⅓ cups (one-half jar) None Such®
  Ready-to-Use Mincemeat
  (Regular or Brandy & Rum)
⅓ cup ReaLime® Lime Juice
  from Concentrate
⅛ teaspoon salt
1 (8-ounce) container Borden® Sour
  Cream, at room temperature
2 tablespoons sugar
½ teaspoon vanilla extract

Preheat oven to 375°. Bake pastry shell
15 minutes. Remove from oven; reduce
oven temperature to 350°. In large mixer
bowl, beat sweetened condensed milk
and eggs. Stir in mincemeat, ReaLime®
brand and salt. Pour into prepared pastry
shell; bake 20 minutes. Meanwhile, in
small bowl, combine sour cream, sugar
and vanilla. Spread evenly over pie.
Return to oven; bake 10 minutes longer.
Cool. Chill 3 hours or until set. Garnish
as desired. Refrigerate leftovers.

AMBROSIA PIE ▲

(Makes one 9-inch pie)

1 (7-ounce) package flaked coconut
  (2⅔ cups), toasted
⅓ cup margarine or butter,
  melted
1 (14-ounce) can Eagle® Brand
  Sweetened Condensed Milk
  (NOT evaporated milk)
⅓ cup ReaLemon® Lemon Juice
  from Concentrate
1 (17-ounce) can fruit cocktail,
  well drained
½ cup slivered almonds, toasted
  and chopped
¼ cup chopped maraschino cherries,
  well drained
1 (4-ounce) container frozen
  non-dairy whipped topping,
  thawed (1¾ cups)
  Additional fruit, optional

Combine coconut and margarine.
Reserving 2 tablespoons coconut mixture,
press remainder firmly on bottom and up
side to rim of 9-inch pie plate. Chill. In
large bowl, combine sweetened condensed milk, ReaLemon® brand, fruit
cocktail, almonds and cherries; mix well.
Fold in whipped topping. Pour into prepared
crust. Garnish with reserved coconut and
additional fruit if desired. Chill 4 hours
or until set. Refrigerate leftovers.

COOKIES & COOKIE BARS

Pictured clockwise from top: Versatile Cut-Out Cookies and Variations: Mincemeat Peek-a-Boo Cookie, Cookie Pecan Critters, Stained Glass Cookies, Chocolate Cookies, Cinnamon Pinwheel Cookies (recipes page 34).

VERSATILE CUT-OUT COOKIES

3½ cups unsifted flour
1 tablespoon baking powder
½ teaspoon salt
1 (14-ounce) can Eagle® Brand Sweetened Condensed Milk (NOT evaporated milk)
¾ cup margarine or butter, softened
2 eggs
1 tablespoon vanilla *or* 2 teaspoons almond *or* lemon extract

Combine flour, baking powder and salt. In large mixer bowl, beat sweetened condensed milk, margarine, eggs and vanilla until well blended. Add dry ingredients; mix well. Chill 2 hours. On floured surface, knead dough to form a smooth ball. Divide into thirds. On well-floured surface, roll out each portion to ⅛-inch thickness. Cut with floured cookie cutter. Reroll as necessary to use all dough. Place 1 inch apart on greased baking sheets. Bake in preheated 350° oven 7 to 9 minutes or until lightly browned around edges *(do not overbake)*. Cool. Frost and decorate as desired. Store loosely covered at room temperature.

Chocolate Cookies: Decrease flour to 3 cups. Add ½ cup unsweetened cocoa. Proceed as above. (Makes about 8½ dozen)

Sandwich Cookies: Use 2½-inch cookie cutter. Bake as directed. Sandwich 2 cookies together with ready-to-spread frosting. Sprinkle with confectioners' sugar if desired. (Makes about 3 dozen)

Cookie Pecan Critters: For each critter, arrange 3 pecan halves together on ungreased baking sheets. Shape 1 teaspoon dough into 1-inch ball. Press firmly onto center of arranged pecans. Repeat until all dough is used. Bake 12 to 14 minutes. Spread tops with Chocolate Frosting*. (Makes about 6½ dozen)

*Chocolate Frosting: In small saucepan, melt ¼ cup margarine or butter with ¼ cup water. Stir in ½ cup unsweetened cocoa. Remove from heat; beat in 2 cups confectioners' sugar and 1 teaspoon vanilla until smooth. Add additional water for a thinner consistency if desired. (Makes about 1 cup)

(Makes about 6½ dozen 3-inch cookies)

Mincemeat Peek-a-Boo Cookies: Prepare and roll dough as above. Cut into 3-inch rounds. Using sharp knife, cut "X" in center of half the rounds. Place 1 teaspoon mincemeat in center of remaining rounds. Top with cut rounds. Bake 8 to 10 minutes. Cool. Sprinkle with confectioners' sugar if desired. (Makes about 4 dozen)

Stained Glass Cookies: Prepare and roll dough as above. Using 3-inch cookie cutters, cut into desired shapes. Cut out holes for "stained glass" in each cookie with small cutters or knife. Place on aluminum foil-lined baking sheets. Fill holes with crushed hard candies. (If planning to hang cookies, make hole in each cookie in dough near edge with straw.) Bake 6 to 8 minutes or until candy has melted. Cool 10 minutes; remove from foil. (Makes about 8 dozen)

Cinnamon Pinwheel Cookies: Decrease baking powder to 2 teaspoons. Prepare and chill dough as above. Divide into quarters. Roll each quarter of dough into a 16x8-inch rectangle. Brush with melted margarine or butter. Top each with 2 tablespoons sugar combined with ½ teaspoon ground cinnamon. Roll up tightly beginning at 8-inch side. Wrap tightly; freeze until firm, about 20 minutes. Cut into ¼-inch slices. Place on ungreased baking sheets. Bake 12 to 14 minutes or until lightly browned. (Makes about 6½ dozen)

Chocolate Snow Balls: Prepare dough as above for chocolate cookies, increasing eggs to 3; add 1 cup finely chopped nuts. Chill. Shape into 1-inch balls. Roll in confectioners' sugar. Bake 8 to 10 minutes. Roll again in confectioners' sugar. (Makes about 7½ dozen)

BUCKEYE COOKIE BARS ▲

(Makes 24 to 36 bars)

1 (18¼- or 18½-ounce) package
  chocolate cake mix
¼ cup vegetable oil
1 egg
1 cup chopped peanuts
1 (14-ounce) can Eagle® Brand
  Sweetened Condensed Milk
  (NOT evaporated milk)
½ cup peanut butter

Preheat oven to 350° (325° for glass dish).
In large mixer bowl, combine cake mix,
oil and egg; beat on medium speed until
crumbly. Stir in peanuts. Reserving
1½ cups crumb mixture, press remainder
firmly on bottom of greased 13x9-inch
baking pan. In medium bowl, beat sweetened condensed milk with peanut butter
until smooth; spread over prepared crust.
Sprinkle with reserved crumb mixture.
Bake 25 to 30 minutes or until set. Cool.
Cut into bars. Store loosely covered at
room temperature.

DOUBLE CHOCOLATE COOKIES ▲

(Makes about 4½ dozen)

2 cups biscuit baking mix
1 (14-ounce) can Eagle® Brand
  Sweetened Condensed Milk
  (NOT evaporated milk)
8 (1-ounce) squares semi-sweet
  chocolate, or 1 (12-ounce) package
  semi-sweet chocolate chips,
  melted
3 tablespoons margarine or butter,
  melted
1 egg
1 teaspoon vanilla extract
6 (1¼-ounce) white candy bars with
  almonds, broken into small pieces
¾ cup chopped nuts

Preheat oven to 350°. In large mixer bowl,
combine all ingredients except candy
pieces and nuts; beat until smooth. Stir
in remaining ingredients. Drop by rounded
teaspoonfuls, 2 inches apart, onto
ungreased baking sheets. Bake 10 minutes or until tops are slightly crusted (do
not overbake). Cool. Store tightly covered
at room temperature.

Mint Chocolate Cookies: Omit white
candy bars. Stir in ¾ cup mint-flavored
chocolate chips. Proceed as above.

ALMOND TOFFEE BARS ▲

(Makes 24 to 36 bars)

1½   cups unsifted flour
½   cup confectioners' sugar
¾   cup cold margarine or butter
1   (14-ounce) can Eagle® Brand
     Sweetened Condensed Milk
     (NOT evaporated milk)
1   egg, beaten
1   teaspoon almond extract
6   (1³⁄₁₆-ounce) milk chocolate-
     covered English toffee candy
     bars, cut into small pieces
1   cup slivered almonds

Preheat oven to 350° (325° for glass dish).
In medium bowl, combine flour and sugar;
cut in margarine until crumbly. Press firmly
on bottom of 13x9-inch baking pan. Bake
15 minutes. Meanwhile, in large bowl,
combine sweetened condensed milk, egg
and extract; mix well. Stir in toffee pieces
and almonds. Spread evenly over prepared crust. Bake 25 minutes or until
golden brown. Cool. Cut into bars. Store
covered in refrigerator.

FUDGE NUT BROWNIES ▲

(Makes 24 to 36 bars)

1   (12-ounce) package semi-sweet
     chocolate chips
¼   cup margarine or butter
2   cups biscuit baking mix
1   (14-ounce) can Eagle® Brand
     Sweetened Condensed Milk
     (NOT evaporated milk)
1   egg, beaten
1   teaspoon vanilla extract
1   to 1½ cups coarsely chopped
     walnuts
     Confectioners' sugar

Preheat oven to 350°. In large saucepan,
over low heat, melt *1 cup* chips with
margarine; remove from heat. Add biscuit
mix, sweetened condensed milk, egg
and vanilla. Stir in nuts and remaining
chips. Turn into well-greased 13x9-inch
baking pan. Bake 20 to 25 minutes or
until brownies begin to pull away from
sides of pan. Cool. Sprinkle with confectioners' sugar. Cut into bars. Store tightly
covered at room temperature.

MARBLED CHEESECAKE BARS ▲

(Makes 24 to 36 bars)

2 cups finely crushed creme-filled chocolate sandwich cookies (about 24 cookies)
3 tablespoons margarine or butter, melted
3 (8-ounce) packages cream cheese, softened
1 (14-ounce) can Eagle® Brand Sweetened Condensed Milk (NOT evaporated milk)
3 eggs
2 teaspoons vanilla extract
2 (1-ounce) squares unsweetened chocolate, melted

Preheat oven to 300°. Combine crumbs and margarine; press firmly on bottom of 13x9-inch baking pan. In large mixer bowl, beat cheese until fluffy. Gradually beat in sweetened condensed milk until smooth. Add eggs and vanilla; mix well. Pour half the batter evenly over prepared crust. Stir melted chocolate into remaining batter; spoon over vanilla batter. With table knife or metal spatula, gently swirl through batter to marble. Bake 45 to 50 minutes or until set. Cool. Chill. Cut into bars. Store covered in refrigerator.

CRUNCHY PEANUT BRICKLE BARS ▲

(Makes 36 to 48 bars)

2 cups quick-cooking oats
1½ cups unsifted flour
1 cup chopped dry-roasted peanuts
1 cup firmly packed brown sugar
1 teaspoon baking soda
½ teaspoon salt
1 cup margarine or butter, melted
1 (14-ounce) can Eagle® Brand Sweetened Condensed Milk (NOT evaporated milk)
½ cup peanut butter
1 (6-ounce) package almond brickle chips, or 6 (1³⁄₁₆-ounce) milk chocolate-covered English toffee candy bars, cut into small pieces

Preheat oven to 375°. In large bowl, combine oats, flour, peanuts, sugar, baking soda and salt; stir in margarine until crumbly. Reserving 1½ cups crumb mixture, press remainder on bottom of greased 15x10-inch jellyroll pan. Bake 12 minutes. Meanwhile, in small mixer bowl, beat sweetened condensed milk with peanut butter until smooth; spread evenly over prepared crust to within ¼ inch of edge. In medium bowl, combine reserved crumb mixture and brickle chips. Sprinkle evenly over peanut butter mixture; press down firmly. Bake 20 minutes or until golden brown. Cool. Cut into bars. Store loosely covered at room temperature.

37

DATE NUT BARS

(Makes 36 to 48 bars)

½ cup margarine or butter, melted
1 (16.6-ounce) package date or nut quick bread mix
1 (14-ounce) can Eagle® Brand Sweetened Condensed Milk (NOT evaporated milk)
1½ cups chopped nuts
1 cup chopped dates
2 eggs
¼ cup orange juice
2 teaspoons grated orange rind
¼ teaspoon salt
Orange Glaze

Preheat oven to 350°. In large bowl, combine all ingredients except Orange Glaze; mix well. Pour into greased and floured 15x10-inch jellyroll pan. Bake 25 minutes or until golden. Cool. Top with Orange Glaze. Cut into bars. Store covered at room temperature.

Orange Glaze: In small bowl, combine 1½ cups confectioners' sugar, 3 tablespoons orange juice and 2 teaspoons grated orange rind; mix until smooth. (Makes about ½ cup)

Cranberry Nut Bars: Omit date quick bread mix and dates. Add 1 (16-ounce) package cranberry quick bread mix and 2 cups fresh or frozen cranberries, finely chopped. Proceed as above. Bake 30 to 35 minutes or until golden. Cool. Top with confectioners' sugar or Orange Glaze.

COOKIE BAR MAKING HINT

For easy clean-up and cutting of bars, line pan with aluminum foil, extending foil over ends of pan. Prepare bars as directed. Cool completely. Lift from pan; fold down foil. Cut into bars. Store as directed.

Pictured from top: Cranberry Nut Bars, Date Nut Bar.

COCONUT MACAROONS

(Makes about 4 dozen)

- **2** (7-ounce) packages *flaked* coconut (5⅓ cups)
- **1** (14-ounce) can Eagle® Brand Sweetened Condensed Milk (NOT evaporated milk)
- **2** teaspoons vanilla extract
- **1½** teaspoons almond extract

Preheat oven to 350°. In large bowl, combine coconut, sweetened condensed milk and extracts; mix well. Drop by rounded teaspoonfuls onto aluminum foil-lined and *generously greased* baking sheets; garnish as desired. Bake 8 to 10 minutes or until lightly browned around edges. *Immediately* remove from baking sheets (macaroons will stick if allowed to cool). Store loosely covered at room temperature.

Macaroon Kisses: Prepare and bake as above. Press solid milk chocolate candy star or drop in center of each macaroon immediately after baking.

Tip: To reduce cost, omit 1 (7-ounce) package coconut and substitute 2 cups fresh bread crumbs (4 slices).

CRANBERRY CHEESE BARS

(Makes 24 to 36 bars)

- **2** cups unsifted flour
- **1½** cups oats
- **¾** cup plus 1 tablespoon firmly packed brown sugar
- **1** cup margarine or butter, softened
- **1** (8-ounce) package cream cheese, softened
- **1** (14-ounce) can Eagle® Brand Sweetened Condensed Milk (NOT evaporated milk)
- **¼** cup ReaLemon® Lemon Juice from Concentrate
- **2** tablespoons cornstarch
- **1** (16-ounce) can whole berry cranberry sauce

Preheat oven to 350°. In large mixer bowl, combine flour, oats, *¾ cup* sugar and margarine; mix until crumbly. Reserving 1½ cups crumb mixture, press remainder firmly on bottom of greased 13x9-inch baking pan. Bake 15 minutes. Meanwhile, in small mixer bowl, beat cheese until fluffy. Gradually beat in sweetened condensed milk until smooth; stir in ReaLemon® brand. Spread evenly over prepared crust. In small bowl, combine remaining *1 tablespoon* sugar and cornstarch; stir in cranberry sauce. Spoon evenly over cheese layer. Top with reserved crumb mixture. Bake 40 minutes or until golden. Cool. Chill. Store covered in refrigerator.

Macaroon Kisses, Cranberry Cheese Bar

MAGIC COOKIE BARS

(Makes 24 to 36 bars)

- ½ cup margarine or butter
- 1½ cups graham cracker crumbs
- 1 (14-ounce) can Eagle® Brand Sweetened Condensed Milk (NOT evaporated milk)
- 1 (6-ounce) package semi-sweet chocolate chips (1 cup)
- 1 (3½-ounce) can flaked coconut (1⅓ cups)
- 1 cup chopped nuts

Preheat oven to 350° (325° for glass dish). In 13x9-inch baking pan, melt margarine in oven. Sprinkle crumbs over margarine; pour sweetened condensed milk evenly over crumbs. Top with remaining ingredients; press down firmly. Bake 25 to 30 minutes or until lightly browned. Cool. Chill if desired. Cut into bars. Store loosely covered at room temperature.

Seven Layer Magic Cookie Bars: Add 1 (6-ounce) package butterscotch flavored chips after chocolate chips.

Double Chocolate Magic Cookie Bars: Increase chocolate chips to 1 (12-ounce) package.

CHOCO-DIPPED PEANUT BUTTER COOKIES

(Makes about 5 dozen)

- 1 (14-ounce) can Eagle® Brand Sweetened Condensed Milk (NOT evaporated milk)
- ¾ to 1 cup peanut butter
- 1 egg
- 1 teaspoon vanilla extract
- 2 cups biscuit baking mix
- 1 pound chocolate-flavored candy coating*, melted

Preheat oven to 350°. In large mixer bowl, beat sweetened condensed milk, peanut butter, egg and vanilla until smooth. Add biscuit mix; mix well. Chill at least 1 hour. Shape into 1-inch balls. Place 2 inches apart on ungreased baking sheets. Bake 10 to 12 minutes or until *lightly* browned *(do not overbake)*. Cool. Partially dip cookies into warm melted candy coating. Place on wax paper-lined baking sheets. Let stand until firm. Store tightly covered at room temperature.

*Also called confectioners' or summer coating—see page 102.

Magic Cookie Bars, Choco-Dipped Peanut Butter Cookies

PETITE MACAROON CUPS ▲

(Makes about 4 dozen)

- 1 cup margarine or butter, softened
- 2 (3-ounce) packages cream cheese, softened
- 2 cups unsifted flour
- 1 (14-ounce) can Eagle® Brand Sweetened Condensed Milk (NOT evaporated milk)
- 2 eggs, beaten
- 1½ teaspoons vanilla extract
- ½ teaspoon almond extract
- 1 (3½-ounce) can flaked coconut (1⅓ cups)

In large mixer bowl, beat margarine and cheese until fluffy; stir in flour. Cover; chill 1 hour. Divide dough into quarters. On floured surface, shape 1 quarter into a smooth ball. Divide into 12 balls. Place each ball in a 1¾-inch muffin cup; press evenly on bottom and up side of each cup. Repeat with remaining dough. In medium bowl, combine sweetened condensed milk, eggs and extracts; mix well. Stir in coconut. Fill muffin cups ¾ full. Bake in preheated 375° oven 16 to 18 minutes or until lightly browned. Cool in pans; remove. Store loosely covered at room temperature.

Chocolate Macaroon Cups: Beat ¼ cup unsweetened cocoa into egg mixture; proceed as above.

FUDGY BROWNIE BARS ▲

(Makes 24 to 36 bars)

- 1¼ cups unsifted flour
- ¼ cup sugar
- ½ cup cold margarine or butter
- 1 (14-ounce) can Eagle® Brand Sweetened Condensed Milk (NOT evaporated milk)
- ¼ cup unsweetened cocoa
- 1 egg
- 1 teaspoon vanilla extract
- ½ teaspoon baking powder
- 1 (8-ounce) bar milk chocolate candy, broken into small pieces
- ¾ cup chopped nuts

Preheat oven to 350°. In medium bowl, combine *1 cup* flour and sugar; cut in margarine until crumbly. Press on bottom of 13x9-inch baking pan. Bake 15 minutes. In large mixer bowl, beat sweetened condensed milk, cocoa, egg, remaining *¼ cup* flour, vanilla and baking powder. Stir in chocolate pieces and nuts. Spread over prepared crust. Bake 20 minutes or until center is set. Cool. Sprinkle with confectioners' sugar if desired. Store tightly covered at room temperature.

Mocha Brownie Bars: Omit milk chocolate candy bar. Increase cocoa to ½ cup. Add 2 tablespoons coffee-flavored liqueur, or 1 teaspoon instant coffee dissolved in 1 tablespoon hot water, to batter. Proceed as above.

41

LEMON CRUMB BARS

(Makes 36 to 48 bars)

- 1 (18¼-ounce) package lemon or yellow cake mix
- ½ cup margarine or butter, softened
- 1 egg plus 3 egg yolks
- 2 cups finely crushed saltine crackers (¼ pound)
- 1 (14-ounce) can Eagle® Brand Sweetened Condensed Milk (NOT evaporated milk)
- ½ cup ReaLemon® Lemon Juice from Concentrate
  Yellow food coloring, optional

Preheat oven to 350°. In large mixer bowl, combine cake mix, margarine and *1 egg*; mix well (mixture will be crumbly). Stir in saltine crumbs. Reserving 2 cups crumb mixture, press remainder firmly on bottom of greased 15x10-inch jellyroll pan. Bake 15 minutes. Meanwhile, in medium bowl, combine *3 egg yolks*, sweetened condensed milk, ReaLemon® brand and food coloring if desired; mix well. Spread evenly over prepared crust. Top with reserved crumb mixture. Bake 15 to 20 minutes or until firm. Cool. Cut into bars. Store covered at room temperature.

CHOCOLATE PECAN BARS

(Makes 24 to 36 bars)

- 1¼ cups unsifted flour
- 1 cup confectioners' sugar
- ⅓ cup unsweetened cocoa
- 1 cup cold margarine or butter
- 1 (14-ounce) can Eagle® Brand Sweetened Condensed Milk (NOT evaporated milk)
- 1 egg
- 2 teaspoons vanilla extract
- 1½ cups chopped pecans

Preheat oven to 350° (325° for glass dish). In large bowl, combine flour, sugar and cocoa; cut in margarine until crumbly. Press firmly on bottom of 13x9-inch baking pan. Bake 15 minutes. Meanwhile, in medium bowl, combine sweetened condensed milk, egg and vanilla; mix well. Stir in nuts. Spread evenly over crust. Bake 25 minutes or until lightly browned. Cool. Cut into bars. Store covered in refrigerator.

Lemon Crumb Bar, Chocolate Pecan Bar

APPLE NUT BARS ▲

(Makes 36 to 48 bars)

4 medium all-purpose apples,
   cored and finely chopped
1 (15.4-ounce) package nut or
   date quick bread mix
1 (14-ounce) can Eagle® Brand
   Sweetened Condensed Milk
   (NOT evaporated milk)
1 cup chopped nuts
3 eggs
2 teaspoons vanilla extract
1½ teaspoons ground cinnamon
½ teaspoon ground nutmeg
   Cream Cheese Frosting

Preheat oven to 350°. In large bowl,
combine all ingredients except frosting;
mix well. Pour into greased and floured
15x10-inch jellyroll pan. Bake 30 minutes
or until golden. Cool. Spread with Cream
Cheese Frosting. Cut into bars. Garnish as
desired. Store covered in refrigerator.

Cream Cheese Frosting: In small mixer
bowl, beat 2 (3-ounce) packages cream
cheese, ½ cup margarine or butter, softened,
and 1 teaspoon vanilla until fluffy. Add
4 cups sifted confectioners' sugar; mix
well. (Makes about 2½ cups)

CALIFORNIA FRUIT BARS ▲

(Makes 24 to 36 bars)

½ cup unsifted flour
1 cup oats
¾ cup firmly packed brown sugar
¼ cup wheat germ
½ cup margarine or butter, softened
2 teaspoons vanilla extract
1½ cups chopped walnuts
1 cup golden raisins
1 (6-ounce) package dried
   apricots, chopped (1 cup)
1 (14-ounce) can Eagle® Brand
   Sweetened Condensed Milk
   (NOT evaporated milk)

Preheat oven to 350° (325° for glass
dish). In large bowl, combine flour, oats,
sugar, wheat germ, margarine and vanilla;
mix until crumbly. Reserving ½ cup crumb
mixture, press remainder on bottom of
greased 13x9-inch baking pan. In large
bowl, combine nuts, raisins, apricots and
sweetened condensed milk; spoon evenly
over crust. Top with reserved crumb
mixture; press down firmly. Bake 25 minutes or until edges are lightly browned.
Cool. Cut into bars. Store covered at
room temperature.

43

CHOCOLATE ALMOND BROWNIES

(Makes 16 brownies)

1¼ cups unsifted flour
2 tablespoons sugar
½ cup cold margarine or butter
1 cup chopped almonds, toasted
1 (14-ounce) can Eagle® Brand Sweetened Condensed Milk (NOT evaporated milk)
¼ cup unsweetened cocoa
1 egg
2 tablespoons amaretto liqueur, or 1 teaspoon almond extract
½ teaspoon baking powder
6 (1¼-ounce) white candy bars with almonds, broken into small pieces

Preheat oven to 350°. In medium bowl, combine 1 cup flour and sugar; cut in margarine until crumbly. Add ¼ cup nuts. Press on bottom of 9-inch round or square baking pan. Bake 15 minutes. In large mixer bowl, beat sweetened condensed milk, remaining ¼ cup flour, cocoa, egg, amaretto and baking powder until smooth. Stir in candy pieces and ½ cup nuts. Spread over prepared crust. Top with remaining ¼ cup nuts. Bake 30 minutes or until center is set. Cool. Cut into wedges. Store tightly covered at room temperature.

CHOCOLATE MINT CHEESECAKE BARS

(Makes 24 to 36 bars)

1¼ cups unsifted flour
1 cup confectioners' sugar
½ cup unsweetened cocoa
¼ teaspoon baking soda
1 cup cold margarine or butter
1 (8-ounce) package cream cheese, softened
1 (14-ounce) can Eagle® Brand Sweetened Condensed Milk (NOT evaporated milk)
2 eggs
1½ teaspoons peppermint extract
Green or red food coloring, optional
Chocolate Glaze

Preheat oven to 350°. In large bowl, combine flour, sugar, cocoa and baking soda; cut in margarine until crumbly (mixture will be dry). Press firmly on bottom of 13x9-inch baking pan. Bake 15 minutes. Meanwhile, in large mixer bowl, beat cheese until fluffy. Gradually beat in sweetened condensed milk until smooth. Add eggs, extract and food coloring if desired; mix well. Pour over prepared crust. Bake 20 minutes or until lightly browned around edges. Cool. Drizzle with Chocolate Glaze. Chill. Cut into bars. Store covered in refrigerator.

Chocolate Glaze: In small saucepan, over low heat, melt 2 (1-ounce) squares semi-sweet chocolate with 2 tablespoons margarine or butter; stir until smooth. Remove from heat; stir in ½ teaspoon vanilla extract. Immediately drizzle over bars. (Makes about ¼ cup)

STREUSEL CARAMEL BARS

(Makes 24 to 36 bars)

2 cups unsifted flour
¾ cup firmly packed light brown sugar
1 egg, beaten
¾ cup cold margarine or butter
¾ cup chopped nuts
24 caramels, unwrapped
1 (14-ounce) can Eagle® Brand Sweetened Condensed Milk (NOT evaporated milk)

Preheat oven to 350°. In large bowl, combine flour, sugar and egg; cut in ½ cup margarine until crumbly. Stir in nuts. Reserving 2 cups crumb mixture, press remainder firmly on bottom of greased 13x9-inch baking pan. Bake 15 minutes. Meanwhile, in heavy saucepan, over low heat, melt caramels with sweetened condensed milk and remaining ¼ cup margarine. Pour over prepared crust. Top with reserved crumb mixture. Bake 20 minutes or until bubbly. Cool. Cut into bars. Store loosely covered at room temperature.

Chocolate Caramel Bars: Melt 2 (1-ounce) squares unsweetened chocolate with caramels, sweetened condensed milk and margarine. Proceed as above.

Pictured from top: Chocolate Almond Brownie, Chocolate Mint Cheesecake Bar, Streusel Caramel Bar.

Fudgy Cookie Wedge, Chocolate Streusel Bar

FUDGY COOKIE WEDGES

(Makes 36 wedges)

1 (20-ounce) package refrigerated cookie dough, any flavor
1 (12-ounce) package semi-sweet chocolate chips
2 tablespoons margarine or butter
1 (14-ounce) can Eagle® Brand Sweetened Condensed Milk (NOT evaporated milk)
1 teaspoon vanilla extract
   Chopped nuts

Preheat oven to 350°. Divide cookie dough into thirds. With floured hands, press on bottom of 3 aluminum foil-lined 9-inch round cake pans or press into 9-inch circles on ungreased baking sheets. Bake 10 to 12 minutes or until golden. Cool. In heavy saucepan, over medium heat, melt chips and margarine with sweetened condensed milk. Cook and stir until thickened, about 5 minutes; add vanilla. Spread over cookie circles. Top with nuts. Chill. Cut into wedges. Store loosely covered at room temperature.

MICROWAVE: Bake cookie dough as above. In 1-quart glass measure, combine remaining ingredients except nuts. Cook on 100% power (high) 4 minutes, stirring after each minute. Proceed as above.

CHOCOLATE STREUSEL BARS

(Makes 24 to 36 bars)

- 1¾ cups unsifted flour
- 1½ cups confectioners' sugar
- ½ cup unsweetened cocoa
- 1 cup cold margarine or butter
- 1 (8-ounce) package cream cheese, softened
- 1 (14-ounce) can Eagle® Brand Sweetened Condensed Milk (NOT evaporated milk)
- 1 egg
- 2 teaspoons vanilla extract
- ½ cup chopped nuts

Preheat oven to 350°. In large bowl, combine flour, sugar and cocoa. Cut in margarine until crumbly (mixture will be dry). Reserving 2 cups crumb mixture, press remainder firmly on bottom of 13x9-inch baking pan. Bake 15 minutes. In large mixer bowl, beat cheese until fluffy. Gradually beat in sweetened condensed milk until smooth. Add egg and vanilla; mix well. Pour over prepared crust. Combine nuts with reserved crumb mixture; sprinkle over cheese mixture. Bake 25 minutes or until bubbly. Cool. Chill. Cut into bars. Store covered in refrigerator.

CHEESECAKE TOPPED BROWNIES

(Makes 36 to 40 bars)

- 1 (21.5- or 23.6-ounce) package fudge brownie mix
- 1 (8-ounce) package cream cheese, softened
- 2 tablespoons margarine or butter, softened
- 1 tablespoon cornstarch
- 1 (14-ounce) can Eagle® Brand Sweetened Condensed Milk (NOT evaporated milk)
- 1 egg
- 2 teaspoons vanilla extract
  Ready-to-spread chocolate frosting, optional

Preheat oven to 350°. Prepare brownie mix as package directs. Spread into well-greased 13x9-inch baking pan. In small mixer bowl, beat cheese, margarine and cornstarch until fluffy. Gradually beat in sweetened condensed milk then egg and vanilla until smooth. Pour evenly over brownie batter. Bake 45 minutes or until top is lightly browned. Cool. Spread with frosting if desired. Cut into bars. Store covered in refrigerator.

Cheesecake Topped Brownies

PUDDINGS & DESSERTS

Pictured clockwise from top left: Strawberry Banana Trifle, Lemon Chiffon Loaf, Granola Cherry Cheese Square (recipes page 50).

STRAWBERRY BANANA TRIFLE

(Makes 10 to 12 servings)

1 (14-ounce) can Eagle® Brand Sweetened Condensed Milk (NOT evaporated milk)
1 cup cold water
1 (4-serving size) package *instant* vanilla flavor pudding mix
2 cups (1 pint) Borden® Whipping Cream, stiffly whipped
1 pint fresh strawberries, cleaned, hulled and sliced
2 bananas, sliced and dipped in ReaLemon® Lemon Juice from Concentrate
1 (10¾- or 12-ounce) prepared loaf pound cake, cut in 12 slices
  Additional strawberries and banana slices

In large bowl, combine sweetened condensed milk and water. Add pudding mix; beat well. Chill 5 minutes. Fold in whipped cream then strawberries and bananas. Line side and bottom of 3½-quart glass serving bowl with cake slices. Spoon pudding mixture into prepared bowl. Cover; chill. Garnish with additional strawberries and banana slices. Refrigerate leftovers.

GRANOLA CHERRY CHEESE SQUARES

(Makes 6 to 9 servings)

2 cups granola, crushed
¼ cup slivered almonds, toasted and chopped
¼ cup margarine or butter, melted
1 (8-ounce) package cream cheese, softened
1 (14-ounce) can Eagle® Brand Sweetened Condensed Milk (NOT evaporated milk)
⅓ cup ReaLemon® Lemon Juice from Concentrate
1 teaspoon almond extract
1 (21-ounce) can cherry pie filling, chilled

Preheat oven to 350°. Combine granola, almonds and margarine; mix well. Placing *1 cup* granola mixture in small baking pan, press remainder on bottom of 9-inch square baking pan. Bake both pans 10 minutes; cool. In large mixer bowl, beat cheese until fluffy. Gradually beat in sweetened condensed milk until smooth. Stir in ReaLemon® brand and almond extract. Pour into prepared 9-inch square baking pan. Top with toasted granola mixture. Chill. Serve with pie filling. Refrigerate leftovers.

LEMON CHIFFON LOAF

(Makes 8 to 10 servings)

24 ladyfinger halves
1 (14-ounce) can Eagle® Brand Sweetened Condensed Milk (NOT evaporated milk)
⅓ cup ReaLemon® Lemon Juice from Concentrate
  Yellow food coloring, optional
3 egg whites*
¼ teaspoon cream of tartar
1 cup (½ pint) Borden® Whipping Cream, stiffly whipped

Line bottom and sides of 9x5-inch loaf pan with aluminum foil, extending foil 1 inch beyond edges of pan. Line sides of pan with *18 ladyfinger halves*. In large bowl, combine sweetened condensed milk, ReaLemon® brand and food coloring if desired; mix well. In small mixer bowl, beat egg whites with cream of tartar until stiff but not dry; fold into sweetened condensed milk mixture. Fold in whipped cream. Pour into prepared pan. Cover filling with remaining *6 ladyfinger halves*. Cover; chill or freeze 4 hours or until set. Invert onto serving plate; peel off foil. Garnish as desired. Refrigerate leftovers.

*Use only Grade A clean, uncracked eggs.

DUTCH APPLE DESSERT

(Makes 6 to 8 servings)

5 medium all-purpose apples,
pared, cored and sliced
1 (14-ounce) can Eagle® Brand
Sweetened Condensed Milk
(NOT evaporated milk)
1 teaspoon ground cinnamon
½ cup plus 2 tablespoons cold
margarine or butter
1½ cups biscuit baking mix
½ cup firmly packed brown sugar
½ cup chopped nuts

Preheat oven to 325°. In medium bowl, combine apples, sweetened condensed milk and cinnamon. In large bowl, cut *½ cup* margarine into *1 cup* biscuit mix until crumbly. Stir in apple mixture. Pour into greased 9-inch square baking pan. In small bowl, combine remaining *½ cup* biscuit mix and sugar; cut in remaining *2 tablespoons* margarine until crumbly. Add nuts. Sprinkle evenly over apple mixture. Bake 1 hour or until golden. Serve warm with ice cream if desired.

MICROWAVE: In 2-quart round baking dish, prepare as above. Cook on 100% power (high) 14 to 15 minutes, rotating dish after 7 minutes. Let stand 5 minutes.

Dutch Apple Dessert

CREAMY RICE PUDDING ▲

(Makes 4 to 6 servings)

2½ cups water
½ cup uncooked long grain rice
1 cinnamon stick or ¼ teaspoon
ground cinnamon
2 (½-inch) pieces lemon rind
Dash salt
1 (14-ounce) can Eagle® Brand
Sweetened Condensed Milk
(NOT evaporated milk)
Additional ground cinnamon

In medium saucepan, combine water, rice, cinnamon, lemon rind and salt; let stand 30 minutes. Bring to a boil, stirring occasionally. Add sweetened condensed milk; mix well. Return to a boil; stir. Reduce heat to medium. Cook uncovered, stirring frequently, 20 to 25 minutes *or until liquid is absorbed to top of rice.* Cool (pudding thickens as it cools). Remove cinnamon stick and lemon rind. Sprinkle with additional cinnamon. Serve warm or chilled. Refrigerate leftovers.

CITRUS-FILLED MERINGUES

(Makes 10 servings)

10 (3-inch) Meringue Shells
 1 (14-ounce) can Eagle® Brand
    Sweetened Condensed Milk
    (NOT evaporated milk)
 ½ cup frozen limeade concentrate,
    thawed
 2 tablespoons ReaLemon® Lemon
    Juice from Concentrate
 2 egg yolks
    Green or yellow food coloring,
    optional
 1 (4-ounce) container frozen non-
    dairy whipped topping,
    thawed (1¾ cups)

Prepare Meringue Shells in advance. In
medium saucepan, combine sweetened
condensed milk, limeade concentrate,
ReaLemon® brand and egg yolks; mix
well. Over medium heat, cook and stir
rapidly until hot and slightly thickened.
Remove from heat; cool 15 minutes. Chill
thoroughly, about 30 minutes. Stir in food
coloring if desired. Fold in whipped topping. Spoon into Meringue Shells; chill.
Garnish as desired. Refrigerate leftovers.

Meringue Shells: Preheat oven to 225°.
Cover baking sheets with ungreased
brown paper. On paper, draw 10 (3-inch)
circles about 2 inches apart; set aside.
In large mixer bowl, combine 6 egg whites,
at room temperature, 1 teaspoon vanilla
extract, ¼ teaspoon cream of tartar and
¼ teaspoon salt. On medium speed, beat
until soft peaks form. On high speed,
gradually beat in 1 cup sugar until stiff
but not dry. With pastry bag and star tip,
pipe meringue within circles on paper
forming shells or spoon within the circles,
forming a hollow in each. Bake 1 hour.
Turn off oven; leave meringues in oven
1 hour.

VANILLA MINT CREAM PUFFS

(Makes 12 servings)

12 Cream Puffs
 1 (14-ounce) can Eagle® Brand
    Sweetened Condensed Milk
    (NOT evaporated milk)
 2 tablespoons white creme
    de menthe
 2 tablespoons cold water
 1 (4-serving size) package *instant*
    vanilla flavor pudding mix
 1 cup (½ pint) Borden® Whipping
    Cream, *stiffly whipped*
    Confectioners' sugar
    Hot Fudge Sauce, optional
    (page 110)

Prepare Cream Puffs in advance. In large
bowl, combine sweetened condensed milk,
liqueur and water. Add pudding mix;
beat well. Chill 5 minutes. Fold in whipped
cream. Chill. Just before serving, fill
cream puffs; sprinkle with confectioners'
sugar. Serve with Hot Fudge Sauce if
desired. Refrigerate leftovers.

Pictured left to right: Vanilla Mint Cream Puff, Citrus-Filled Meringue, Strawberries Romanoff.

Cream Puffs: In medium saucepan, heat 1 cup water and ½ cup margarine or butter to a rolling boil. Stir in 1 cup unsifted flour. Reduce heat to low; stir rapidly until mixture forms a ball, about 1 minute. Remove from heat. Add 4 eggs; beat until smooth. Using about ¼ cup dough for each, drop 3 inches apart onto ungreased baking sheets. Bake in preheated 400° oven 35 to 40 minutes or until puffed and golden. Cool. To serve, split and remove any dough from centers of puffs.

Chocolate Mint Cream Puffs: Beat 1 (1-ounce) square unsweetened chocolate, melted, with sweetened condensed milk. Substitute *instant* chocolate flavor pudding mix for vanilla. Proceed as above.

STRAWBERRIES ROMANOFF

(Makes 10 to 12 servings)

1 (14-ounce) can Eagle® Brand
  Sweetened Condensed Milk
  (NOT evaporated milk)
¾ cup cold water
3 to 4 tablespoons orange-flavored
  liqueur or kirsch
  Yellow food coloring, optional
1 (4-serving size) package *instant*
  vanilla flavor pudding mix
2 cups (1 pint) Borden® Whipping
  Cream, *stiffly whipped*
1 quart fresh strawberries, cleaned,
  hulled and sliced (about 4 cups)

In large bowl, combine sweetened condensed milk, water, liqueur and food coloring if desired; mix well. Add pudding mix; beat well. Chill 15 minutes. Fold in whipped cream. Cover; chill. Just before serving, reserve *1 cup* strawberries; fold in remaining strawberries. Garnish with reserved strawberries. Refrigerate leftovers.

CREAMY BANANA PUDDING

1 (14-ounce) can Eagle® Brand Sweetened Condensed Milk (NOT evaporated milk)
1½ cups cold water
1 (4-serving size) package *instant* vanilla flavor pudding mix
2 cups (1 pint) Borden® Whipping Cream, whipped
36 vanilla wafers
3 medium bananas, sliced and dipped in ReaLemon® Lemon Juice from Concentrate

In large bowl, combine sweetened condensed milk and water. Add pudding mix; beat well. Chill 5 minutes. Fold in whipped cream. Spoon *1 cup* pudding mixture into 2½-quart glass serving bowl. Top with one-third *each* of the wafers, bananas and pudding. Repeat layering twice, ending with pudding. Cover; chill. Garnish as desired. Refrigerate leftovers.

Tip: Mixture can be layered in individual serving dishes.

PISTACHIO PINEAPPLE DESSERT

(Makes 12 to 15 servings)

2 cups shortbread cookie crumbs
(about 30 cookies), *or* vanilla
wafer crumbs (about 50 wafers)

½ cup plus 3 tablespoons shelled,
chopped pistachio nuts or pecans

¼ cup margarine or butter, melted

1 (8-ounce) package cream
cheese, softened

1 (14-ounce) can Eagle® Brand
Sweetened Condensed Milk
(NOT evaporated milk)

¼ cup ReaLime® Lime Juice
from Concentrate

1 (4-serving size) package *instant*
pistachio flavor pudding mix

1 (8-ounce) can crushed pineapple,
undrained

1 cup (½ pint) Borden® Whipping
Cream, whipped

Preheat oven to 350°. Combine crumbs, *3 tablespoons* nuts and margarine; press firmly on bottom of 9-inch springform pan *or* 13x9-inch baking pan. Bake 8 to 10 minutes. Cool. Meanwhile, in large mixer bowl, beat cheese until fluffy. Gradually beat in sweetened condensed milk then ReaLime® brand and pudding mix until smooth. Stir in remaining *½ cup* nuts and pineapple. Fold in whipped cream. Pour into prepared pan. Chill 6 hours or overnight. Garnish as desired. Refrigerate leftovers.

FRENCH APPLE BREAD PUDDING

(Makes 6 to 9 servings)

- 3 eggs
- 1 (14-ounce) can Eagle® Brand Sweetened Condensed Milk (NOT evaporated milk)
- 3 medium all-purpose apples, pared, cored and finely chopped
- 1¾ cups hot water
- ¼ cup margarine or butter, melted
- 1 teaspoon ground cinnamon
- 1 teaspoon vanilla extract
- 4 cups French bread cubes (about 6 ounces)
- ½ cup raisins, optional

Preheat oven to 350°. In large bowl, beat eggs; add sweetened condensed milk, apples, water, margarine, cinnamon and vanilla. Stir in bread and raisins, moistening completely. Turn into buttered 9-inch square baking pan. Bake 1 hour or until knife inserted near center comes out clean. Cool. Serve warm with ice cream if desired. Refrigerate leftovers.

GOLDEN BREAD PUDDING

(Makes 6 to 9 servings)

- 4 cups soft white bread cubes (5 slices)
- 3 eggs
- 1 teaspoon ground cinnamon
- 3 cups warm water
- 1 (14-ounce) can Eagle® Brand Sweetened Condensed Milk (NOT evaporated milk)
- 2 tablespoons margarine or butter, melted
- 2 teaspoons vanilla extract
- ½ teaspoon salt
  Butter Rum Sauce

Preheat oven to 350°. Place bread cubes in buttered 9-inch square baking pan. In large bowl, beat eggs and cinnamon; add remaining ingredients except Butter Rum Sauce. Pour evenly over bread, moistening completely. Bake 45 to 50 minutes or until knife inserted in center comes out clean. Cool. Serve warm with Butter Rum Sauce. Refrigerate leftovers.

Tip: For a softer, more custard-like bread pudding, decrease bread cubes to 3 cups.

Butter Rum Sauce: In saucepan, melt ¼ cup butter or margarine; add ¾ cup firmly packed brown sugar and ½ cup Borden® Whipping Cream. Boil rapidly 8 to 10 minutes; add 2 tablespoons rum or 1 teaspoon rum flavoring. Serve warm. (Makes about 1 cup)

Banana Bread Pudding: Substitute whole wheat bread cubes for white bread cubes. Add ½ cup flaked coconut. Decrease water to 2½ cups. Beat 3 ripe medium bananas, mashed, with eggs. Proceed as above. Top with ½ cup chopped pecans. Bake as above. Serve with Butter Rum Sauce.

CHOCOLATE CINNAMON BREAD PUDDING

(Makes 6 to 9 servings)

- 4 cups soft white bread cubes (5 slices)
- ½ cup chopped nuts
- 3 eggs
- ¼ cup unsweetened cocoa
- 2 teaspoons vanilla extract
- 1 teaspoon ground cinnamon
- ½ teaspoon salt
- 1 (14-ounce) can Eagle® Brand Sweetened Condensed Milk (NOT evaporated milk)
- 2¾ cups water
- 2 tablespoons margarine or butter, melted
  Cinnamon Cream Sauce

Preheat oven to 350°. Place bread cubes and nuts in buttered 9-inch square baking pan. In large bowl, beat eggs, cocoa, vanilla, cinnamon and salt. Add sweetened condensed milk, water and margarine; mix well. Pour evenly over bread, moistening completely. Bake 40 to 45 minutes or until knife inserted in center comes out clean. Cool slightly. Serve warm with Cinnamon Cream Sauce. Refrigerate leftovers.

Cinnamon Cream Sauce: In medium saucepan, combine 1 cup (½ pint) Borden® Whipping Cream, ⅔ cup firmly packed brown sugar, 1 teaspoon vanilla extract and ½ teaspoon ground cinnamon. Bring to a boil; reduce heat and boil rapidly 6 to 8 minutes or until thickened, stirring occasionally. Serve warm. (Makes about 1 cup)

Pictured from top: Banana Bread Pudding, French Apple Bread Pudding, Chocolate Cinnamon Bread Pudding.

FLUFFY YOGURT FRUIT DESSERTS

(Makes 8 to 10 servings)

1 (14-ounce) can Eagle® Brand Sweetened Condensed Milk (NOT evaporated milk)
1 (8-ounce) container Borden® Lite-line® Fruit Yogurt, any flavor
2 tablespoons ReaLemon® Lemon Juice from Concentrate
  Food coloring, optional
2 cups fresh fruit
1 (8-ounce) container frozen non-dairy whipped topping, thawed (3½ cups)
  Additional fruit

In large bowl, combine all ingredients except whipped topping and additional fruit; mix well. Fold in whipped topping. Spoon into individual serving dishes. Chill. Just before serving, garnish with additional fruit. Refrigerate leftovers.

FRESH FRUIT AMBROSIA

(Makes 10 to 12 servings)

1 (14-ounce) can Eagle® Brand Sweetened Condensed Milk (NOT evaporated milk)
1 (8-ounce) container Borden® Lite-line® Orange Yogurt
½ cup ReaLime® Lime Juice from Concentrate
3 oranges, peeled and sectioned
2 cups fresh pineapple chunks
1½ cups grape halves (about ½ pound)
1 (3½-ounce) can flaked coconut (1⅓ cups)
1 cup Campfire® Miniature Marshmallows
1 cup chopped pecans

In large bowl, combine sweetened condensed milk, yogurt and ReaLime® brand; mix well. Stir in remaining ingredients. Chill at least 3 hours to blend flavors. Garnish as desired. Refrigerate leftovers.

CARAMEL FLAN

¾ cup sugar
4 eggs
1¾ cups water
1 (14-ounce) can Eagle® Brand
  Sweetened Condensed Milk
  (NOT evaporated milk)
½ teaspoon vanilla extract
⅛ teaspoon salt

Preheat oven to 350°. In heavy skillet, over medium heat, cook sugar, stirring constantly until melted and caramel-colored. Pour into ungreased 1½-quart ring mold* or 9-inch round or square baking pan, tilting to coat bottom completely. In medium bowl, beat eggs; stir in water, sweetened condensed milk, vanilla and salt. Pour over caramelized sugar; set pan in larger pan (a broiler pan). Fill larger pan with 1 inch hot water. Bake 55 to 60 minutes or until knife inserted near center comes out clean. Cool. Chill. Loosen side of flan with knife; invert onto serving plate with rim. Garnish as desired. Refrigerate leftovers.

*If using ring mold, decrease sugar to ⅓ cup.

CHEESECAKES

Pictured clockwise from left: Fudge
Truffle Cheesecake (recipe page 63),
Cherries Jubilee Cheesecake (recipe
page 62), Chocolate Chip Cheesecake
(recipe page 62).

CHOCOLATE CHIP CHEESECAKE

(Makes one 9-inch cheesecake)

1½ cups finely crushed creme-
    filled chocolate sandwich
    cookies (about 18 cookies)
2   to 3 tablespoons margarine or
    butter, melted
3   (8-ounce) packages cream
    cheese, softened
1   (14-ounce) can Eagle® Brand
    Sweetened Condensed Milk
    (NOT evaporated milk)
3   eggs
2   teaspoons vanilla extract
1   cup mini chocolate chips
1   teaspoon flour

Preheat oven to 300°. Combine crumbs
and margarine; press firmly on bottom of
9-inch springform pan or 13x9-inch baking
pan. In large mixer bowl, beat cheese
until fluffy. Gradually beat in sweetened
condensed milk until smooth. Add eggs
and vanilla; mix well. In small bowl, toss
½ cup chips with flour to coat; stir into
cheese mixture. Pour into prepared pan.
Sprinkle remaining ½ cup chips evenly
over top. Bake 1 hour or until center
springs back when lightly touched.
Cool. Chill. Garnish as desired.
Refrigerate leftovers.

CHERRIES JUBILEE CHEESECAKE

(Makes one 9-inch cheesecake)

1¼ cups graham cracker crumbs
¼   cup plus 1 tablespoon sugar
⅓   cup margarine or butter, melted
3   (8-ounce) packages cream
    cheese, softened
1   (14-ounce) can Eagle® Brand
    Sweetened Condensed Milk
    (NOT evaporated milk)
4   eggs
¼   cup kirsch or other cherry-
    flavored liqueur
1½ teaspoons almond extract
1   (17-ounce) can pitted dark sweet
    cherries, drained, reserving
    syrup
1   tablespoon flour
2   teaspoons cornstarch

Preheat oven to 300°. Combine crumbs,
¼ cup sugar and margarine; press firmly
on bottom of 9-inch springform pan. In
large mixer bowl, beat cheese until fluffy.
Gradually beat in sweetened condensed
milk until smooth. Add eggs, 3 tablespoons kirsch and 1 teaspoon extract;
mix well. Chop ½ cup cherries; toss with
flour. Stir into cheese mixture. Pour into
prepared pan. Bake 1 hour and 10 minutes
or until center is set. Cool. Chill. In small
saucepan, combine cornstarch and
remaining 1 tablespoon sugar. Stir
in reserved cherry syrup, remaining

CHEESECAKE MAKING HINTS

- A springform pan (with removable side and bottom) is the most commonly
  used pan for making baked cheesecakes.
- For best distribution of added ingredients (chocolate chips, raisins, nuts, etc.)
  or for even marbling, do not oversoften or overbeat cream cheese.
- To minimize cracking:
    - Avoid overbeating batter.
    - Avoid overbaking.
    - After baking, turn off oven and allow cheesecake to cool in oven with
      door slightly open. If removed from oven, cool away from drafts.
    - During cooling, run a knife tip around the edge of pan so that the cake
      can pull away freely as it contracts.
- Cool to room temperature before chilling thoroughly.
- After cheesecake is completely cooled, gently loosen cheesecake from pan
  side with the tip of a knife or narrow spatula while slowly releasing pan clamp.
  Carefully remove side of pan.
- Ungarnished baked cheesecakes freeze well.

1 *tablespoon* kirsch and ½ *teaspoon* extract. Over medium heat, cook and stir until thickened. Cool. Cut remaining cherries in half; add to sauce. Chill. Serve with cheesecake. Refrigerate leftovers.

FUDGE TRUFFLE CHEESECAKE

(Makes one 9-inch cheesecake)

Chocolate Crumb Crust
3 (8-ounce) packages cream cheese, softened
1 (14-ounce) can Eagle® Brand Sweetened Condensed Milk (NOT evaporated milk)
1 (12-ounce) package semi-sweet chocolate chips, *or* 8 (1-ounce) squares semi-sweet chocolate, melted
4 eggs
¼ cup coffee-flavored liqueur, optional
2 teaspoons vanilla extract

Preheat oven to 300°. Prepare Chocolate Crumb Crust. In large mixer bowl, beat cheese until fluffy. Gradually beat in sweetened condensed milk until smooth. Add remaining ingredients; mix well. Pour into prepared pan. Bake 1 hour and 5 minutes or until center is set. Cool. Chill. Garnish as desired. Refrigerate leftovers.

Chocolate Crumb Crust: In medium bowl, combine 1½ cups vanilla wafer crumbs (about 45 wafers), 6 tablespoons confectioners' sugar, ⅓ cup unsweetened cocoa and ⅓ cup margarine or butter, melted. Press firmly on bottom and ½ inch up side of 9-inch springform pan.

ALMOND PRALINE CHEESECAKE

(Makes one 9-inch cheesecake)

¾ cup graham cracker crumbs
½ cup slivered almonds, toasted and finely chopped
¼ cup firmly packed brown sugar
¼ cup margarine or butter, melted
3 (8-ounce) packages cream cheese, softened
1 (14-ounce) can Eagle® Brand Sweetened Condensed Milk (NOT evaporated milk)
3 eggs
1 teaspoon almond extract
Almond Praline Topping

Almond Praline Cheesecake

Preheat oven to 300°. Combine crumbs, nuts, sugar and margarine; press firmly on bottom of 9-inch springform pan *or* 13x9-inch baking pan. In large mixer bowl, beat cheese until fluffy. Gradually beat in sweetened condensed milk until smooth. Add eggs and extract; mix well. Pour into prepared pan. Bake 55 to 60 minutes or until center is set. Cool. Top with Almond Praline Topping. Chill. Refrigerate leftovers.

Almond Praline Topping: In small saucepan, combine ⅓ cup firmly packed dark brown sugar and ⅓ cup Borden® Whipping Cream. Cook and stir until sugar dissolves. Simmer 5 minutes or until thickened. Remove from heat; stir in ½ cup chopped toasted slivered almonds. Spoon evenly over cake. (For 13x9-inch pan, double all topping ingredients; simmer 10 to 12 minutes or until thickened.)

TRIPLE CHOCOLATE & VANILLA CHEESECAKE

(Makes one 9-inch cheesecake)

1½ cups finely crushed creme-
   filled chocolate sandwich
   cookies (about 18 cookies)
3 tablespoons margarine or butter,
   melted
4 (8-ounce) packages cream
   cheese, softened
1 (14-ounce) can Eagle® Brand
   Sweetened Condensed Milk
   (NOT evaporated milk)
4 eggs
⅓ cup unsifted flour
1 tablespoon vanilla extract
2 (1-ounce) squares semi-sweet
   chocolate, melted
   Chocolate Glaze

Preheat oven to 350°. Combine crumbs
and margarine; press firmly on bottom of
9-inch springform pan. In large mixer
bowl, beat cheese until fluffy. Gradually
beat in sweetened condensed milk until
smooth. Add eggs, flour and vanilla; mix
well. Divide batter in half. Add chocolate
to one half of batter; mix well. Pour into
prepared pan. Top evenly with vanilla
batter. Bake 50 to 55 minutes or until
center springs back when lightly touched.
Cool. Top with Chocolate Glaze. Chill.
Refrigerate leftovers.

Chocolate Glaze: In small saucepan,
over low heat, melt 2 (1-ounce) squares
semi-sweet chocolate with ¼ cup Borden®
Whipping Cream. Cook and stir until
thickened and smooth. Remove from heat;
spread over cheesecake. (Makes about
⅓ cup)

Tip: Glaze can be doubled.

APPLE CINNAMON CHEESECAKE

(Makes one 9-inch cheesecake)

½ cup plus 1 tablespoon margarine or butter, softened
¼ cup firmly packed light brown sugar
1 cup unsifted flour
¼ cup quick-cooking oats
¼ cup finely chopped walnuts
½ teaspoon ground cinnamon
2 (8-ounce) packages cream cheese, softened
1 (14-ounce) can Eagle® Brand Sweetened Condensed Milk (NOT evaporated milk)
3 eggs
½ cup frozen apple juice concentrate, thawed
2 medium all-purpose apples, cored and sliced
Cinnamon Apple Glaze

Preheat oven to 300°. In small mixer bowl, beat ½ cup margarine and sugar until fluffy. Add flour, oats, nuts and cinnamon; mix well. Press firmly on bottom and half-way up side of 9-inch springform pan. Bake 10 minutes. Meanwhile, in large mixer bowl, beat cheese until fluffy. Gradually beat in sweetened condensed milk until smooth. Add eggs and juice concentrate; mix well. Pour into prepared pan. Bake 45 minutes or until center springs back when lightly touched. Cool. In large skillet, cook apples in remaining 1 tablespoon margarine until tender-crisp. Arrange on top of cheesecake; drizzle with Cinnamon Apple Glaze. Chill. Refrigerate leftovers.

Cinnamon Apple Glaze: In small sauce-pan, combine ¼ cup frozen apple juice concentrate, thawed, 1 teaspoon corn-starch and ¼ teaspoon ground cinnamon; mix well. Over low heat, cook and stir until thickened. (Makes about ¼ cup)

FROZEN PEPPERMINT CHEESECAKE ▲

(Makes one 9-inch cheesecake)

1¼ cups chocolate wafer cookie crumbs (about 24 wafers)
¼ cup sugar
¼ cup margarine or butter, melted
1 (8-ounce) package cream cheese, softened
1 (14-ounce) can Eagle® Brand Sweetened Condensed Milk (NOT evaporated milk)
1 cup crushed hard peppermint candy
  Red food coloring, optional
2 cups (1 pint) Borden® Whipping Cream, whipped

Combine crumbs, sugar and margarine; press firmly on bottom and halfway up side of 9-inch springform pan. In large mixer bowl, beat cheese until fluffy. Gradually beat in sweetened condensed milk until smooth. Stir in crushed candy and food coloring if desired. Fold in whipped cream. Pour into prepared pan; cover. Freeze 6 hours or until firm. Garnish as desired. Freeze leftovers.

GERMAN CHOCOLATE CHEESECAKE SQUARES ▲

(Makes one 15x10-inch cheesecake)

1½ cups graham cracker crumbs
½ cup sugar
½ cup margarine or butter, melted
3 (8-ounce) packages cream cheese, softened
1 (14-ounce) can Eagle® Brand Sweetened Condensed Milk (NOT evaporated milk)
2 (4-ounce) packages sweet cooking chocolate, melted
3 eggs
1 tablespoon vanilla extract
  Coconut Pecan Topping

Preheat oven to 350°. Combine crumbs, sugar and margarine; press firmly on bottom of 15x10-inch jellyroll pan. In large mixer bowl, beat cheese until fluffy. Gradually beat in sweetened condensed milk until smooth. Add remaining ingredients except Coconut Pecan Topping; mix well. Pour into prepared pan. Bake 20 minutes or until center is set. Cool. Top with Coconut Pecan Topping. Chill. Refrigerate leftovers.

Coconut Pecan Topping: In heavy saucepan, combine 1 (14-ounce) can Eagle®

Brand Sweetened Condensed Milk (NOT evaporated milk) and 3 egg yolks; mix well. Add ½ cup margarine or butter. Over medium-low heat, cook and stir until thickened and bubbly, 8 to 10 minutes. Remove from heat; stir in 1 (3½-ounce) can flaked coconut (1⅓ cups), 1 cup chopped pecans and 1 teaspoon vanilla. Cool 10 minutes. (Makes about 2¾ cups)

MAPLE PUMPKIN CHEESECAKE

(Makes one 9-inch cheesecake)

- 1¼ **cups graham cracker crumbs**
- ¼ **cup sugar**
- ¼ **cup margarine or butter, melted**
- 3 **(8-ounce) packages cream cheese, softened**
- 1 **(14-ounce) can Eagle® Brand Sweetened Condensed Milk (NOT evaporated milk)**
- 1 **(16-ounce) can pumpkin (2 cups)**
- 3 **eggs**
- 1 **cup Cary's®, Vermont Maple Orchards or MacDonald's Pure Maple Syrup**
- 1½ **teaspoons ground cinnamon**
- 1 **teaspoon ground nutmeg**
- ½ **teaspoon salt**
  Maple Pecan Glaze

Preheat oven to 300°. Combine crumbs, sugar and margarine; press firmly on bottom of 9-inch springform pan or 13x9-inch baking pan. In large mixer bowl, beat cheese until fluffy. Gradually beat in sweetened condensed milk until smooth. Add pumpkin, eggs, ¼ cup maple syrup, cinnamon, nutmeg and salt; mix well. Pour into prepared pan. Bake 1 hour and 15 minutes or until edge springs back when lightly touched (center will be slightly soft). Cool. Chill. Top with Maple Pecan Glaze. Refrigerate leftovers.

Maple Pecan Glaze: In saucepan, combine remaining ¾ cup maple syrup and 1 cup (½ pint) Borden® Whipping Cream; bring to a boil. Boil rapidly 15 to 20 minutes or until thickened; stir occasionally. Add ½ cup chopped pecans. (Makes about 1¼ cups)

Maple Pumpkin Cheesecake

MINI CHEESECAKES

(Makes about 2 dozen)

1½ cups graham cracker or chocolate wafer crumbs
¼ cup sugar
¼ cup margarine or butter, melted
3 (8-ounce) packages cream cheese, softened
1 (14-ounce) can Eagle® Brand Sweetened Condensed Milk (NOT evaporated milk)
3 eggs
2 teaspoons vanilla extract

Preheat oven to 300°. Combine crumbs, sugar and margarine; press equal portions onto bottoms of 24 lightly greased* or paper-lined muffin cups. In large mixer bowl, beat cheese until fluffy. Gradually beat in sweetened condensed milk until smooth. Add eggs and vanilla; mix well. Spoon equal amounts of mixture (about 3 tablespoons) into prepared cups. Bake 20 minutes or until cakes spring back when lightly touched. Cool. Chill. Garnish as desired. Refrigerate leftovers.

Chocolate Mini Cheesecakes: Add 1 (6-ounce) package semi-sweet chocolate chips (1 cup), melted, to batter; mix well. Proceed as above. Bake 20 to 25 minutes.

*If greased muffin cups are used, cool baked cheesecakes. Freeze 15 minutes; remove from pans. Proceed as above.

CREAMY BAKED CHEESECAKE

(Makes one 9-inch cheesecake)

1¼ cups graham cracker crumbs
¼ cup sugar
⅓ cup margarine or butter, melted
2 (8-ounce) packages cream
    cheese, softened
1 (14-ounce) can Eagle® Brand
    Sweetened Condensed Milk
    (NOT evaporated milk)
3 eggs
¼ cup ReaLemon® Lemon Juice
    from Concentrate
1 (8-ounce) container Borden® Sour
    Cream, at room temperature
    Raspberry Topping, optional

Preheat oven to 300°. Combine crumbs, sugar and margarine; press firmly on bottom of 9-inch springform pan. In large mixer bowl, beat cheese until fluffy. Gradually beat in sweetened condensed milk until smooth. Add eggs and ReaLemon® brand; mix well. Pour into prepared pan. Bake 50 to 55 minutes or until center is set; top with sour cream. Bake 5 minutes longer. Cool. Chill. Serve with Raspberry Topping if desired. Refrigerate leftovers.

Raspberry Topping: In small saucepan, combine ⅔ cup syrup drained from 1 (10-ounce) package thawed frozen red raspberries, ¼ cup red currant jelly or red raspberry jam and 1 tablespoon cornstarch. Cook and stir until slightly thickened and clear. Cool. Stir in raspberries. (Makes about 1⅓ cups)

New York Style Cheesecake: Omit sour cream. Increase cream cheese to 4 (8-ounce) packages and eggs to 4. Add 2 tablespoons flour after eggs. Proceed as above. Bake 1 hour and 10 minutes or until center is set. Cool. Chill. Serve as above if desired.

MICROWAVE CHEESECAKE

(Makes one 10-inch cheesecake)

⅓ cup margarine or butter
1¼ cups graham cracker crumbs
¼ cup sugar
2 (8-ounce) packages cream cheese, softened
1 (14-ounce) can Eagle® Brand Sweetened Condensed Milk (NOT evaporated milk)
3 eggs
¼ cup ReaLemon® Lemon Juice from Concentrate
1 (8-ounce) container Borden® Sour Cream, at room temperature

In 10-inch microwaveable quiche dish or pie plate, melt margarine loosely covered on 100% power (high) 1 minute. Add crumbs and sugar; press firmly on bottom of dish. Cook on 100% power (high) 1½ minutes, rotating dish once. In 2-quart glass measure, beat cheese until fluffy. Gradually beat in sweetened condensed milk until smooth. Add eggs then ReaLemon® brand; mix well. Cook on 70% power (medium-high) 6 to 8 minutes or until hot, stirring every 2 minutes. Pour into prepared dish. Cook on 50% power (medium) 6 to 8 minutes or until center is set, rotating dish once. Top with sour cream. Cool. Chill. Serve with fruit if desired. Refrigerate leftovers.

WALNUT RUM RAISIN CHEESECAKE

(Makes one 9-inch cheesecake)

1 cup raisins
2 tablespoons rum, *or* water plus
　　½ teaspoon rum flavoring
1 cup graham cracker crumbs
½ cup finely chopped walnuts
¼ cup sugar
¼ cup margarine or butter, melted
3 (8-ounce) packages cream
　　cheese, softened
1 (14-ounce) can Eagle® Brand
　　Sweetened Condensed Milk
　　(NOT evaporated milk)
3 eggs
　Walnut Praline Glaze

Preheat oven to 300°. In small bowl, combine raisins and rum; set aside. Combine crumbs, nuts, sugar and margarine; press firmly on bottom of 9-inch springform pan *or* 13x9-inch baking pan. In large mixer bowl, beat cheese until fluffy. Gradually beat in sweetened condensed milk until smooth. Add eggs; mix well. Drain rum from raisins; stir rum into batter. Pour into prepared pan. Top evenly with raisins. Bake 55 to 60 minutes or until center is set. Cool. Top with Walnut Praline Glaze. Chill. Refrigerate leftovers.

Walnut Praline Glaze: In small saucepan, combine ⅓ cup firmly packed dark brown sugar and ⅓ cup Borden® Whipping Cream. Cook and stir until sugar dissolves. Bring to a boil; reduce heat and simmer 5 minutes or until thickened. Remove from heat; stir in ¾ cup chopped toasted walnuts. Spoon over cake. (For 13x9-inch pan, double all glaze ingredients; simmer 10 to 12 minutes or until thickened.)

ORANGE BANANA CHEESECAKE

(Makes one 9-inch cheesecake)

1½ cups vanilla wafer crumbs
   (about 36 wafers)
¼ cup margarine or butter, melted
3 (8-ounce) packages cream
   cheese, softened
1 (14-ounce) can Eagle® Brand
   Sweetened Condensed Milk
   (NOT evaporated milk)
1 banana, mashed (about ½ cup)
¼ cup frozen orange juice
   concentrate, thawed
3 eggs
1 teaspoon grated orange rind
   Fresh orange sections and
   banana slices
   Orange Glaze

Preheat oven to 300°. Combine crumbs and margarine; press firmly on bottom of 9-inch springform pan. In large mixer bowl, beat cheese until fluffy. Gradually beat in sweetened condensed milk until smooth. Add banana, juice concentrate, eggs and rind; mix well. Pour into prepared pan. Bake 55 to 60 minutes or until center is set. Cool. Top with orange sections and banana slices then Orange Glaze. Chill. Garnish as desired. Refrigerate leftovers.

Orange Glaze: In small saucepan, combine ¼ cup sugar and 2½ teaspoons cornstarch; add ½ cup orange juice and ¼ teaspoon grated orange rind. Over medium heat, cook and stir until thickened. Remove from heat; cool. (Makes about ½ cup)

FROZEN MOCHA CHEESECAKE LOAF

(Makes 8 to 10 servings)

- 2 cups finely crushed creme-filled chocolate sandwich cookies (about 20 cookies)
- 3 tablespoons margarine or butter, melted
- 1 (8-ounce) package cream cheese, softened
- 1 (14-ounce) can Eagle® Brand Sweetened Condensed Milk (NOT evaporated milk)
- 1 tablespoon vanilla extract
- 2 cups (1 pint) Borden® Whipping Cream, whipped
- 2 tablespoons instant coffee dissolved in 1 tablespoon hot water
- ½ cup chocolate-flavored syrup

Line 9x5-inch loaf pan with aluminum foil, extending foil above sides of pan. Combine crumbs and margarine; press firmly on bottom and halfway up sides of prepared pan. In large mixer bowl, beat cheese until fluffy. Gradually beat in sweetened condensed milk until smooth; add vanilla. Fold in whipped cream. Remove half the mixture and place in medium bowl; fold in coffee liquid and chocolate syrup. Spoon half the chocolate mixture into prepared pan then half the vanilla mixture. Repeat. With table knife, cut through cream mixture to marble. Cover; freeze 6 hours or until firm. To serve, remove from pan; peel off foil. Garnish as desired. Slice to serve. Freeze leftovers.

AMARETTO CHEESECAKE

(Makes one 9-inch cheesecake)

- ¾ cup graham cracker crumbs
- ½ cup slivered almonds, toasted and finely chopped
- ¼ cup sugar
- ¼ cup margarine or butter, melted
- 3 (8-ounce) packages cream cheese, softened
- 1 (14-ounce) can Eagle® Brand Sweetened Condensed Milk (NOT evaporated milk)
- 2 eggs
- ¼ cup amaretto liqueur
  Chocolate Amaretto Glaze

Preheat oven to 300°. Combine crumbs, nuts, sugar and margarine; press firmly on bottom of 9-inch springform pan. In large mixer bowl, beat cheese until fluffy. Gradually beat in sweetened condensed milk until smooth. Add eggs and amaretto; mix well. Pour into prepared pan. Bake 55 to 60 minutes or until center is set. Cool. Drizzle with Chocolate Amaretto Glaze. Chill. Refrigerate leftovers.

Chocolate Amaretto Glaze: In small saucepan, over low heat, melt 1 (1-ounce) square unsweetened chocolate with 1 tablespoon margarine or butter and dash salt, stirring constantly until smooth. Remove from heat. Stir in ¾ cup confectioners' sugar, 3 to 4 teaspoons boiling water and 1½ teaspoons amaretto. Stir until smooth and well blended. *Immediately* drizzle or spread over cheesecake. (Makes about ⅓ cup)

PUMPKIN ORANGE CHEESECAKE

(Makes one 9-inch cheesecake)

- 1½ cups gingersnap cookie crumbs (about 32 cookies)
- ¼ cup margarine or butter, melted
- 3 (8-ounce) packages cream cheese, softened
- 1 (14-ounce) can Eagle® Brand Sweetened Condensed Milk (NOT evaporated milk)
- 1 (16-ounce) can pumpkin (2 cups)
- 2 eggs
- 3 tablespoons orange-flavored liqueur or orange juice
- 1 teaspoon pumpkin pie spice
- ¼ teaspoon salt

Preheat oven to 300°. Combine crumbs and margarine; press firmly on bottom and halfway up side of 9-inch springform pan. In large mixer bowl, beat cheese until fluffy. Gradually beat in sweetened condensed milk until smooth. Add remaining ingredients; mix well. Pour into prepared pan. Bake 1 hour and 15 minutes or until edge springs back when lightly touched (center will be slightly soft). Cool. Chill. Garnish as desired. Refrigerate leftovers.

TROPICAL CHEESECAKE

(Makes one 9-inch cheesecake)

- 1¼ cups graham cracker crumbs
- ½ cup flaked coconut, toasted
- ½ cup toasted, finely chopped nuts
- 2 tablespoons light brown sugar
- ¼ cup margarine or butter, melted
- 2 (8-ounce) packages cream cheese, softened
- 1 (14-ounce) can Eagle® Brand Sweetened Condensed Milk (NOT evaporated milk)
- 3 eggs
- ¼ cup frozen orange juice concentrate, thawed
- 1 (20-ounce) can juice-pack crushed pineapple, well drained, reserving ½ cup juice
- 1 (8-ounce) container Borden® Sour Cream, at room temperature
- 2 tablespoons granulated sugar
- 1½ teaspoons cornstarch

Preheat oven to 300°. Combine crumbs, coconut, nuts, brown sugar and margarine; press firmly on bottom and halfway up side of 9-inch springform pan. In large mixer bowl, beat cheese until fluffy. Gradually beat in sweetened condensed milk until smooth. Add eggs and juice concentrate; mix well. Stir in ¾ cup pineapple. Pour into prepared pan. Bake 1 hour and 5 minutes or until center is set; spread top with sour cream. Bake 5 minutes longer. Cool. Meanwhile, in small saucepan, combine granulated sugar and cornstarch; mix well. Gradually add reserved pineapple juice then pineapple. Over low heat, cook and stir until thickened. Cool. Spread over cheesecake. Chill. Garnish as desired. Refrigerate leftovers.

Pictured from top on opposite page: Amaretto Cheesecake, Pumpkin Orange Cheesecake. Pictured above: Tropical Cheesecake.

ITALIAN CHEESECAKE

(Makes one 9-inch cheesecake)

- 1¼ cups graham cracker crumbs
- ¼ cup sugar
- ½ teaspoon ground cinnamon
- ⅓ cup margarine or butter, melted
- 2 (15- or 16-ounce) containers ricotta cheese
- 1 (14-ounce) can Eagle® Brand Sweetened Condensed Milk (NOT evaporated milk)
- 4 eggs
- 1 tablespoon vanilla extract
- 2 teaspoons grated orange rind
- 2 tablespoons chopped candied cherries, *or* citron
- 2 to 4 tablespoons golden raisins
- 1 tablespoon flour

Preheat oven to 350°. Combine crumbs, sugar, cinnamon and margarine; press firmly on bottom of 9-inch springform pan. In large mixer bowl, beat cheese and sweetened condensed milk until smooth. Add eggs, vanilla and rind; mix well. In small bowl, toss cherries and raisins with flour to coat; stir into cheese mixture. Pour into prepared pan. Bake 1 hour and 10 minutes or until lightly browned around edge. Cool. Chill. Garnish with confectioners' sugar and ground cinnamon if desired. Refrigerate leftovers.

DOUBLE LEMON CHEESECAKE ▶

(Makes one 9-inch cheesecake)

- 1¼ cups graham cracker crumbs
- ¼ cup sugar
- ⅓ cup margarine or butter, melted
- 4 (8-ounce) packages cream cheese, softened
- 1 (14-ounce) can Eagle® Brand Sweetened Condensed Milk (NOT evaporated milk)
- 4 eggs
- 2 tablespoons flour
- ¼ cup ReaLemon® Lemon Juice from Concentrate
  Lemon Glaze

Preheat oven to 350°. Combine crumbs, sugar and margarine; press firmly on bottom of 9-inch springform pan. In large mixer bowl, beat cheese until fluffy. Gradually beat in sweetened condensed milk until smooth. Add eggs and flour; mix well. Stir in ReaLemon® brand. Pour into prepared pan. Bake 1 hour or until lightly browned. Cool. Top with Lemon Glaze. Chill. Garnish as desired. Refrigerate leftovers.

Lemon Glaze: In small saucepan, combine ⅓ cup sugar, 1 tablespoon cornstarch and dash salt. Add ⅓ cup water, ¼ cup ReaLemon® brand and 1 egg yolk; mix well. Over medium heat, cook and stir until thickened and bubbly. Remove from heat; add 1 tablespoon margarine or butter and yellow food coloring if desired. Stir until well blended. Cool. (Makes about ¾ cup)

Italian Cheesecake

FROZEN PEACH AMARETTO CHEESECAKE

(Makes one 9-inch cheesecake)

- 1 cup graham cracker crumbs
- ¼ cup slivered almonds, toasted and finely chopped
- 2 tablespoons sugar
- ⅓ cup margarine or butter, melted
- 1 (8-ounce) package cream cheese, softened
- 1 (14-ounce) can Eagle® Brand Sweetened Condensed Milk (NOT evaporated milk)
- 2 cups pureed fresh or thawed frozen peaches
- ⅓ cup amaretto liqueur
- 1 cup (½ pint) Borden® Whipping Cream, whipped
  Peach slices and almonds

Combine crumbs, *¼ cup* nuts, sugar and margarine; press firmly on bottom of 9-inch springform pan. In large mixer bowl, beat cheese until fluffy. Gradually beat in sweetened condensed milk until smooth. Stir in pureed peaches and liqueur. Fold in whipped cream. Pour into prepared pan. Cover; freeze 6 hours or until firm. Remove from freezer 5 minutes before serving. Garnish with peach slices and almonds. Freeze leftovers.

77

ICE CREAM & FROZEN DESSERTS

Pictured from left: Frozen Fruit Salad, Fudgy Chocolate Ice Cream, Frozen Piña Colada Torte (recipes page 80).

FROZEN PIÑA COLADA TORTE

(Makes 12 to 15 servings)

1 (7-ounce) package flaked coconut, toasted (2⅔ cups)
3 tablespoons margarine or butter, melted
1 (14-ounce) can Eagle® Brand Sweetened Condensed Milk (NOT evaporated milk)
½ cup Coco Lopez® Cream of Coconut
1 (20-ounce) can crushed pineapple, *well drained*
2 cups (1 pint) Borden® Whipping Cream, whipped *(do not use non-dairy whipped topping)*
Maraschino cherries

Reserving ¾ cup coconut, combine remaining coconut and margarine; press firmly on bottom of 9-inch springform pan, 13x9-inch baking pan *or* 9-inch square pan. In large bowl, combine sweetened condensed milk and cream of coconut; stir in *1 cup* pineapple. Fold in whipped cream. Pour half the mixture into prepared pan. Sprinkle with ½ cup reserved coconut; top with remaining cream mixture. Cover; freeze 6 hours or until firm. Just before serving, garnish with remaining coconut, remaining pineapple and cherries. Freeze leftovers.

FUDGY CHOCOLATE ICE CREAM

(Makes about 1½ quarts)

5 (1-ounce) squares unsweetened chocolate, melted
1 (14-ounce) can Eagle® Brand Sweetened Condensed Milk (NOT evaporated milk)
2 teaspoons vanilla extract
2 cups (1 pint) Borden® Half-and-Half
2 cups (1 pint) Borden® Whipping Cream, *unwhipped*
½ cup chopped nuts, optional

In large mixer bowl, beat chocolate, sweetened condensed milk and vanilla until well blended. Stir in half-and-half, whipping cream and nuts if desired. Pour into ice cream freezer container. Freeze according to manufacturer's instructions. Freeze leftovers.

Refrigerator-Freezer Method: Omit half-and-half. Reduce chocolate to 3 (1-ounce) squares. Whip whipping cream. In large mixer bowl, beat chocolate, sweetened condensed milk and vanilla until well blended; fold in whipped cream and nuts if desired. Pour into 9x5-inch loaf pan or other 2-quart container; cover. Freeze 6 hours or until firm. Freeze leftovers.

FROZEN FRUIT SALAD

(Makes 8 to 10 servings)

1 (3½-ounce) can flaked coconut, lightly toasted (1⅓ cups)
3 tablespoons margarine or butter, melted
1 (17-ounce) can fruit cocktail, *well drained*
1 (14-ounce) can Eagle® Brand Sweetened Condensed Milk (NOT evaporated milk)
1 cup Campfire® Miniature Marshmallows
1 cup chopped pecans
1 (8-ounce) container Borden® Sour Cream
¾ to 1 cup chopped maraschino cherries
½ cup ReaLime® Lime Juice from Concentrate
1 (4-ounce) container frozen non-dairy whipped topping, thawed (1¾ cups)

Line 9x5-inch loaf pan with aluminum foil, extending foil above sides of pan. Combine coconut and margarine; press firmly on bottom of prepared pan. In large bowl, combine remaining ingredients except whipped topping; mix well. Fold in whipped topping. Pour into prepared pan. Freeze 6 hours or until firm. To serve, remove from pan; peel off foil. Garnish as desired. Slice to serve. Freeze leftovers.

RAINBOW ICE CREAMS

(Makes about 1½ quarts)

1 (4-serving size) package fruit-flavored gelatin, any flavor
½ cup *boiling* water
1 (14-ounce) can Eagle® Brand Sweetened Condensed Milk (NOT evaporated milk)
2 cups (1 pint) Borden® Half-and-Half or Coffee Cream
2 cups (1 pint) Borden® Whipping Cream, *unwhipped*
1 cup pureed or mashed fruit, optional
Food coloring, optional

In large bowl, dissolve gelatin in water. Stir in remaining ingredients. Pour into ice cream freezer container. Freeze according to manufacturer's instructions. Freeze leftovers.

Flavor Suggestions:

Lime-Flavored Gelatin: Add 2 tablespoons ReaLime® Lime Juice from Concentrate. Proceed as above.

Lemon-Flavored Gelatin: Add 1 tablespoon grated lemon rind. Proceed as above.

Orange-Flavored Gelatin: Add 1 tablespoon grated orange rind. Proceed as above.

Pictured from top: Orange, Lemon, Lime Rainbow Ice Creams.

RASPBERRY DAIQUIRI PARFAITS

(Makes 8 to 10 servings)

- 1 (14-ounce) can Eagle® Brand Sweetened Condensed Milk (NOT evaporated milk)
- 1 (6-ounce) can frozen raspberry daiquiri mix, thawed
- ¼ to ⅓ cup light rum
- 2 cups (1 pint) Borden® Whipping Cream, whipped *(do not use non-dairy whipped topping)*

In large bowl, combine sweetened condensed milk, daiquiri mix and rum. Fold in whipped cream. Spoon equal portions into 8 to 10 individual serving dishes. Freeze 4 hours or until firm. Garnish as desired. Freeze leftovers.

Peach Daiquiri Parfaits: Substitute 1 (6-ounce) can frozen peach daiquiri mix, thawed, for raspberry; add yellow food coloring if desired. Proceed as above.

Strawberry Daiquiri Parfaits: Substitute 1 (6-ounce) can frozen strawberry daiquiri mix, thawed, for raspberry. Proceed as above.

CHOCOLATE AMARETTO PARFAITS

(Makes 8 to 10 servings)

- 1 (14-ounce) can Eagle® Brand Sweetened Condensed Milk (NOT evaporated milk)
- ⅔ cup chocolate-flavored syrup
- ⅓ cup amaretto liqueur
- 2 tablespoons creme de cacao
- 2 cups (1 pint) Borden® Whipping Cream, whipped *(do not use non-dairy whipped topping)*

In large bowl, combine sweetened condensed milk, chocolate syrup and liqueurs. Fold in whipped cream. Spoon equal portions into 8 to 10 individual serving dishes. Freeze 4 hours or until firm. Garnish as desired. Freeze leftovers.

Raspberry Daiquiri Parfait, Chocolate Amaretto Parfait

FROZEN PASSION

(Makes 2 to 3 quarts)

2 (14-ounce) cans Eagle® Brand
   Sweetened Condensed Milk
   (NOT evaporated milk)
1 (2-liter) bottle or 5 (12-ounce) cans
   carbonated beverage, any flavor

In electric ice cream freezer container,
combine ingredients; mix well. Freeze
according to manufacturer's instructions.
Freeze leftovers.

Frozen Passion Shakes: In blender container, combine one-half (14-ounce) can
Eagle® Brand Sweetened Condensed
Milk, 1 (12-ounce) can carbonated beverage and 3 cups crushed ice. Blend until
smooth. Repeat for additional shakes.
Freeze leftovers. (Makes 1 or 2 quarts)

Frozen Passion Pops: Combine 1 (14-
ounce) can Eagle® Brand Sweetened
Condensed Milk with 2 (12-ounce) cans
carbonated beverage; mix well. Pour equal
portions into 8 (5-ounce) paper cold-drink
cups. Cover each cup with aluminum foil;
make small hole in center of each. Insert
wooden stick into each cup. Freeze 6 hours
or until firm. (Makes 8 servings)

FRESH FRUIT ICE CREAM ▲

(Makes about 1½ quarts)

3 cups (1½ pints) Borden®
   Half-and-Half
1 (14-ounce) can Eagle® Brand
   Sweetened Condensed Milk
   (NOT evaporated milk)
1 cup pureed or mashed fresh fruit
   (peaches, strawberries, bananas,
   raspberries, etc.)
1 tablespoon vanilla extract
   Food coloring, optional

In ice cream freezer container, combine
all ingredients; mix well. Freeze
according to manufacturer's instructions.
Freeze leftovers.

Vanilla Ice Cream: Omit fruit and food
coloring. Increase half-and-half to 4 cups.
Proceed as above.

Refrigerator-Freezer Method: Omit half-
and-half. In large bowl, combine sweetened condensed milk and vanilla; stir
in 1 cup pureed or mashed fruit and food
coloring if desired. Fold in 2 cups (1 pint)
Borden® Whipping Cream, whipped
(do not use non-dairy whipped topping).
Pour into 9x5-inch loaf pan or other
2-quart container; cover. Freeze 6 hours
or until firm. Freeze leftovers.

Strawberry Frozen Passion

BROWNIE MINT SUNDAE SQUARES ▲

(Makes 10 to 12 servings)

1 (21.5- or 23.6-ounce) package fudge brownie mix
1 (14-ounce) can Eagle® Brand Sweetened Condensed Milk (NOT evaporated milk)
2 teaspoons peppermint extract
Green food coloring, optional
2 cups (1 pint) Borden® Whipping Cream, whipped
½ cup mini chocolate chips
Hot Fudge Sauce (page 110)

Prepare brownie mix as package directs. Turn into aluminum foil-lined and greased 13x9-inch baking pan. Bake as directed. Cool thoroughly. In large bowl, combine sweetened condensed milk, extract and food coloring if desired. Fold in whipped cream and chips. Pour over brownie layer. Cover; freeze 6 hours or until firm. To serve, lift from pan with foil; cut into squares. Serve with Hot Fudge Sauce. Freeze leftovers.

PEPPERMINT ICE CREAM GEMS ▲

(Makes 2 dozen)

3 cups finely crushed creme-filled chocolate sandwich cookies (about 34 cookies)
½ cup margarine or butter, melted
1 (14-ounce) can Eagle® Brand Sweetened Condensed Milk (NOT evaporated milk)
¼ cup white creme de menthe or ½ teaspoon peppermint extract
2 tablespoons peppermint schnapps
Red or green food coloring, optional
2 cups (1 pint) Borden® Whipping Cream, whipped (do not use non-dairy whipped topping)

Combine crumbs and margarine. Using back of spoon, press 2 rounded table-spoons crumb mixture in bottom and up side of 24 (2½-inch) paper-lined muffin cups. In large mixer bowl, combine sweet-ened condensed milk, creme de menthe, schnapps and food coloring if desired. Fold in whipped cream. Spoon mixture into prepared cups. Freeze 6 hours or until firm. To serve, remove paper liners. Garnish as desired. Freeze leftovers.

STRAWBERRY SUNDAE DESSERT ▲

(Makes 6 to 9 servings)

1 (8½-ounce) package chocolate wafers, finely crushed (2½ cups crumbs)
½ cup margarine or butter, melted
1 (14-ounce) can Eagle® Brand Sweetened Condensed Milk (NOT evaporated milk)
1 tablespoon vanilla extract
2 cups (1 pint) Borden® Whipping Cream, whipped
2 (10-ounce) packages frozen strawberries in syrup, thawed
¼ cup sugar
1 tablespoon ReaLemon® Lemon Juice from Concentrate
2 teaspoons cornstarch

Combine crumbs and margarine. Press half the crumb mixture on bottom of 9-inch square baking pan. In large bowl, combine sweetened condensed milk and vanilla. Fold in whipped cream. Pour into prepared pan. In blender or food processor, combine strawberries, sugar and ReaLemon® brand; blend until smooth. Spoon ¾ cup strawberry mixture evenly over cream mixture. Top with remaining crumb mixture. Cover; freeze 6 hours or until firm. In small saucepan, combine remaining strawberry mixture and cornstarch. Over medium heat, cook and stir until thickened. Cool. Chill. Cut dessert into squares; serve with sauce. Freeze leftover dessert; refrigerate leftover sauce.

FROZEN LEMON SQUARES ▲

(Makes 6 to 9 servings)

1¼ cups graham cracker crumbs
¼ cup sugar
¼ cup margarine or butter, melted
3 egg yolks*
1 (14-ounce) can Eagle® Brand Sweetened Condensed Milk (NOT evaporated milk)
½ cup ReaLemon® Lemon Juice from Concentrate
Yellow food coloring, optional
Whipped topping or whipped cream

Preheat oven to 350°. Combine crumbs, sugar and margarine; press firmly on bottom of 8- or 9-inch square pan. In small mixer bowl, beat egg yolks, sweetened condensed milk, ReaLemon® brand and food coloring if desired. Pour into prepared pan. Bake 8 minutes. Cool. Top with whipped topping. Freeze 4 hours or until firm. Let stand 10 minutes before serving. Garnish as desired. Freeze leftovers.

Tip: Dessert can be chilled instead of frozen.

*Use only Grade A clean, uncracked eggs.

85

FROZEN AMARETTO TORTE

(Makes 12 to 15 servings)

1 (8½-ounce) package chocolate
   wafers, finely crushed (2½ cups
   crumbs)
½ cup slivered almonds, toasted
   and chopped
⅓ cup margarine or butter, melted
1 (6-ounce) package butterscotch
   flavored chips (1 cup)
1 (14-ounce) can Eagle® Brand
   Sweetened Condensed Milk
   (NOT evaporated milk)
1 (16-ounce) container Borden®
   Sour Cream
⅓ cup amaretto liqueur
1 cup (½ pint) Borden® Whipping
   Cream, whipped

Combine crumbs, almonds and margarine.
Reserving 1¼ cups crumb mixture, press
remainder firmly on bottom of 9-inch
springform pan. In small saucepan, over
medium heat, melt chips with sweetened
condensed milk. In large bowl, combine
sour cream and amaretto; stir in butterscotch mixture. Fold in whipped cream.
Pour half the cream mixture over prepared
crust; top with *1 cup* reserved crumb mixture then remaining cream mixture. Top
with remaining ¼ cup crumb mixture;
cover. Freeze 6 hours or until firm. Garnish
as desired. Freeze leftovers.

FROZEN CHOCOLATE BANANA LOAF

(Makes 8 to 10 servings)

- 1½ cups chocolate wafer cookie crumbs (about 30 wafers)
- ¼ cup sugar
- 3 tablespoons margarine or butter, melted
- 1 (14-ounce) can Eagle® Brand Sweetened Condensed Milk (NOT evaporated milk)
- ⅔ cup chocolate-flavored syrup
- 2 small ripe bananas, mashed (¾ cup)
- 2 cups (1 pint) Borden® Whipping Cream, whipped *(do not use non-dairy whipped topping)*

Line 9x5-inch loaf pan with aluminum foil, extending foil above sides of pan; butter foil. Combine crumbs, sugar and margarine; press firmly on bottom and halfway up sides of prepared pan. In large bowl, combine sweetened condensed milk, chocolate syrup and bananas; mix well. Fold in whipped cream. Pour into prepared pan; cover. Freeze 6 hours or until firm. To serve, remove from pan; peel off foil. Garnish as desired. Slice to serve. Freeze leftovers.

CAKES

Pictured clockwise from left: Fudge Ribbon Cake and Variations: Fudge Ribbon Layer Cake, Fudge Ribbon Cupcakes, Grasshopper Ribbon Cake (recipes page 90).

FUDGE RIBBON CAKE

(Makes one 10-inch cake)

1 (18¼- or 18½-ounce) package
    chocolate cake mix
1 (8-ounce) package cream
    cheese, softened
2 tablespoons margarine or butter,
    softened
1 tablespoon cornstarch
1 (14-ounce) can Eagle® Brand
    Sweetened Condensed Milk
    (NOT evaporated milk)
1 egg
1 teaspoon vanilla extract
    Confectioners' sugar or
    Chocolate Glaze

Preheat oven to 350°. Prepare cake mix as package directs. Pour batter into *well-greased* and floured 10-inch bundt pan. In small mixer bowl, beat cheese, margarine and cornstarch until fluffy. Gradually beat in sweetened condensed milk then egg and vanilla until smooth. Pour evenly over cake batter. Bake 50 to 55 minutes or until wooden pick inserted near center comes out clean. Cool 15 minutes; remove from pan. Cool. Sprinkle with confectioners' sugar or drizzle with Chocolate Glaze.

Chocolate Glaze: In small saucepan, over low heat, melt 1 (1-ounce) square unsweetened or semi-sweet chocolate and 1 tablespoon margarine or butter with 2 tablespoons water. Remove from heat. Stir in ¾ cup confectioners' sugar and ½ teaspoon vanilla extract. Stir until smooth and well blended. (Makes about ⅓ cup)

Fudge Ribbon Sheet Cake: Prepare cake mix as package directs. Pour batter into well-greased and floured 15x10-inch jelly-roll pan. Prepare cream cheese topping as above; spoon evenly over batter. Bake 20 minutes or until wooden pick inserted near center comes out clean. Cool. Frost with 1 (16-ounce) can ready-to-spread chocolate frosting.

Fudge Ribbon Layer Cake: Prepare cake mix as package directs. Pour batter into three well-greased and floured 8- or 9-inch round layer cake pans. Prepare cream cheese topping as above. Spoon equal portions (¾ cup) evenly over batter. Bake 30 to 35 minutes or until wooden pick inserted near center comes out clean. Cool 10 minutes; remove from pans. Cool. Frost with 1 (16-ounce) can ready-to-spread chocolate frosting.

Fudge Ribbon Cupcakes: Prepare cake mix as package directs. Fill 36 paper-lined muffin cups half-full of batter. Prepare cream cheese topping as above; spoon about 2 tablespoonfuls into each cup. Bake 20 minutes or until wooden pick comes out clean. Cool. Frost with 1 (16-ounce) can ready-to-spread chocolate frosting. Garnish as desired.

Grasshopper Ribbon Cake: Prepare cake mix as package directs. Pour batter into any of the above pans. Prepare cheese topping as above, omitting vanilla. Add 2 tablespoons green creme de menthe and a few drops green food coloring if desired. Proceed as above.

JEWELLED FRUITCAKE ▲

(Makes one 10-inch cake)

2½ cups unsifted flour
1 teaspoon baking soda
2 eggs
1 jar None Such® Ready-to-Use
    Mincemeat (Regular or Brandy
    & Rum)
1 (14-ounce) can Eagle® Brand
    Sweetened Condensed Milk
    (NOT evaporated milk)
1 (8-ounce) container green
    candied cherries, halved (1 cup)
1 (8-ounce) container red candied
    cherries, halved (1 cup)
1 (6-ounce) package dried
    apricots, chopped (1 cup)
1 (6-ounce) container candied
    pineapple, chopped (1 cup)
1½ cups chopped pecans

Preheat oven to 300°. Grease and flour
10-inch tube or bundt pan. Combine flour
and baking soda. In large bowl, beat eggs;
stir in remaining ingredients. Blend in dry
ingredients. Pour batter into prepared pan.
Bake 1 hour and 30 to 40 minutes or
until wooden pick inserted near center
comes out clean. Cool 10 minutes; remove
from pan. Cool.

Tip: If desired, glaze with warm corn
syrup; garnish with candied fruit and
dried apricots.

CARAMEL FUDGE CAKE ▲

(Makes one 13x9-inch cake)

1 (18¼- or 18½-ounce) package
    chocolate cake mix
1 (14-ounce) package caramels,
    unwrapped
½ cup margarine or butter
1 (14-ounce) can Eagle® Brand
    Sweetened Condensed Milk
    (NOT evaporated milk)
1 cup coarsely chopped pecans

Preheat oven to 350°. Prepare cake mix
as package directs. Pour 2 cups batter into
greased 13x9-inch baking pan; bake 15
minutes. Meanwhile, in heavy saucepan,
over low heat, melt caramels and margarine. Remove from heat; add sweetened
condensed milk. Mix well. Spread caramel mixture evenly over cake; spread
remaining cake batter over caramel mixture. Top with nuts. Return to oven; bake
30 to 35 minutes longer or until cake
springs back when lightly touched. Cool.
Garnish as desired.

ONE-STEP CHOCOLATE CAKE ROLL

(Makes 8 to 10 servings)

- **1 (14-ounce) can Eagle® Brand Sweetened Condensed Milk (NOT evaporated milk)**
- **2 egg yolks plus 3 eggs**
- **½ cup flaked coconut**
- **½ cup chopped nuts**
- **¼ cup margarine or butter, melted**
- **2 teaspoons vanilla extract**
- **1 cup sugar**
- **⅔ cup unsifted flour**
- **⅓ cup unsweetened cocoa**
- **⅓ cup water**
  Confectioners' sugar
  Chocolate Glaze, optional

Preheat oven to 350°. Line 15x10-inch jellyroll pan with aluminum foil, extending foil 1 inch over ends of pan. Grease aluminum foil. In medium bowl, combine sweetened condensed milk, *2 egg yolks*, coconut, nuts, margarine and *1 teaspoon* vanilla; mix well. Spread evenly into prepared pan. In large mixer bowl, beat *3 eggs* at high speed until fluffy. Gradually beat in sugar then beat 2 minutes. Add remaining ingredients except confectioners' sugar; beat 1 minute. Pour evenly over coconut mixture. Bake 20 to 25 minutes or until cake springs back when lightly touched. Sprinkle generously with confectioners' sugar. *Immediately* turn onto towel. Peel off foil; beginning at narrow end, roll up cake, jellyroll-fashion. Place on serving plate, seam-side down. Cool. Sprinkle with additional confectioners' sugar and drizzle with chocolate glaze if desired.

Chocolate Glaze: In small saucepan, over low heat, melt 2 (1-ounce) squares semi-sweet chocolate with 2 tablespoons margarine or butter; stir until smooth. Remove from heat; stir in ½ teaspoon vanilla extract. Immediately drizzle over cake roll. (Makes about ¼ cup)

DELUXE PINEAPPLE CAKE ▲

(Makes one 13x9-inch cake)

2 (8-ounce) cans juice-pack crushed pineapple, *well drained*, reserving juice
Water
1 (18¼- or 18½-ounce) package yellow cake mix
3 eggs
1 (14-ounce) can Eagle® Brand Sweetened Condensed Milk (NOT evaporated milk)
⅓ cup vegetable oil
1 (3-ounce) package cream cheese, softened
¼ cup frozen pineapple juice concentrate, thawed
Yellow food coloring, optional

Preheat oven to 350°. To reserved pineapple juice, add enough water to make 1 cup. In large mixer bowl, combine cake mix, 1 cup pineapple liquid, eggs, ⅓ cup sweetened condensed milk and oil. Beat on low speed until moistened, then beat on high speed 3 minutes. Stir in 1 can drained pineapple. Pour into well-greased and floured 13x9-inch baking pan. Bake 35 to 40 minutes or until wooden pick inserted near center comes out clean. Cool. Meanwhile, in medium bowl, beat cheese until fluffy. Gradually beat in remaining sweetened condensed milk until smooth. Stir in juice concentrate, food coloring if desired, then remaining 1 can drained pineapple. Chill. Spread evenly over cooled cake. Refrigerate leftovers.

MISSISSIPPI MUD CAKE ▲

(Makes one 13x9-inch cake)

1 (18¼- or 18½-ounce) package chocolate cake mix
1 cup water
3 eggs
½ cup vegetable oil
1 (14-ounce) can Eagle® Brand Sweetened Condensed Milk (NOT evaporated milk)
1 teaspoon ground cinnamon
3 cups Campfire® Miniature Marshmallows
¼ cup margarine or butter
¼ cup unsweetened cocoa
1 cup confectioners' sugar
1 cup chopped pecans
1 teaspoon vanilla extract

Preheat oven to 350°. In large mixer bowl, combine cake mix, water, eggs, oil and ⅓ cup sweetened condensed milk and cinnamon. Beat on low speed until moistened, then beat on high speed 2 minutes. Pour into well-greased and floured 13x9-inch baking pan. Bake 45 minutes or until wooden pick inserted near center comes out clean. Top with marshmallows; bake 2 minutes longer or until marshmallows begin to puff. In saucepan, over medium heat, melt margarine; stir in remaining sweetened condensed milk and cocoa until smooth. Remove from heat. Stir in remaining ingredients. Spoon evenly over warm cake.

PEACH CREAM CAKE

(Makes 10 to 12 servings)

1 (7-inch) prepared loaf angel food
  cake, frozen
1 (14-ounce) can Eagle® Brand
  Sweetened Condensed Milk
  (NOT evaporated milk)
1 cup cold water
1 teaspoon almond extract
1 (4-serving size) package *instant*
  vanilla flavor pudding mix
2 cups (1 pint) Borden® Whipping
  Cream, whipped
4 cups pared, sliced fresh peaches
  (about 2 pounds)

Cut cake into ¼-inch slices; arrange
half the slices on bottom of 13x9-inch
baking dish. In large bowl, combine
sweetened condensed milk, water and
extract. Add pudding mix; beat well.
Chill 5 minutes. Fold in whipped cream.
Pour half the cream mixture over cake
slices; arrange half the peach slices on
top. Repeat layering, ending with peach
slices. Chill 4 hours or until set. Cut into
squares to serve. Refrigerate leftovers.

STRAWBERRY BROWNIE TORTE ▶

(Makes 10 to 12 servings)

1 (21.5- or 23.6-ounce) package fudge
  brownie mix
1 (14-ounce) can Eagle® Brand
  Sweetened Condensed Milk
  (NOT evaporated milk)
½ cup cold water
1 (4-serving size) package *instant*
  vanilla flavor pudding mix
1 (4-ounce) container frozen non-
  dairy whipped topping, thawed
  (1¾ cups)
1 quart fresh strawberries, cleaned,
  hulled and halved

Preheat oven to 350°. Grease two 9-inch
round layer cake pans. Line with wax
paper, extending up sides of pans; grease
wax paper. Prepare brownie mix as package directs for cake-like brownies; pour
into prepared pans. Bake 20 minutes or
until top springs back when touched.
Cool. In large bowl, mix sweetened
condensed milk and water; beat in pudding
mix. Chill 5 minutes. Fold in whipped
topping. Place 1 brownie layer on serving
plate. Top with half *each* the pudding
mixture and strawberries. Repeat. Garnish
as desired. Refrigerate leftovers.

Peach Cream Cake

APPLE SPICE CUSTARD CAKE ▲

(Makes one 13x9-inch cake)

1 (18¼-ounce) package spice cake mix
2 medium all-purpose apples, pared,
   cored and finely chopped
1 (14-ounce) can Eagle® Brand
   Sweetened Condensed Milk
   (NOT evaporated milk)
1 (8-ounce) container Borden®
   Sour Cream, at room temperature
¼ cup ReaLemon® Lemon Juice
   from Concentrate
   Ground cinnamon

Preheat oven to 350°. Prepare cake mix
as package directs; stir in apples. Pour
into well-greased and floured 13x9-inch
baking pan. Bake 30 minutes or until
wooden pick inserted near center comes
out clean. Meanwhile, in medium bowl,
combine sweetened condensed milk,
sour cream and ReaLemon® brand.
Remove cake from oven; spread cream
mixture over top. Return to oven; bake
10 minutes longer or until set. Sprinkle
with cinnamon. Cool. Garnish as desired.
Refrigerate leftovers.

GERMAN CHOCOLATE CAKE ▲

(Makes one 13x9-inch cake)

1 (18¼-ounce) package German
   chocolate cake mix
1 cup water
3 eggs plus 1 egg yolk
½ cup vegetable oil
1 (14-ounce) can Eagle® Brand
   Sweetened Condensed Milk
   (NOT evaporated milk)
3 tablespoons margarine or butter
⅓ cup chopped pecans
⅓ cup flaked coconut
1 teaspoon vanilla extract

Preheat oven to 350°. In large mixer
bowl, combine cake mix, water, 3 eggs,
oil and ⅓ cup sweetened condensed
milk. Beat on low speed until moistened,
then beat on high speed 2 minutes. Pour
into well-greased and floured 13x9-inch
baking pan. Bake 40 to 45 minutes or until
wooden pick inserted near center comes
out clean. In small saucepan, combine
remaining sweetened condensed milk,
egg yolk and margarine. Over medium
heat, cook and stir until thickened, about
6 minutes. Add pecans, coconut and
vanilla; spread over warm cake.

DOUBLE LEMON CAKE　▲

(Makes one 13x9-inch cake)

1 (18¼- or 18½-ounce) package
lemon cake mix
1 (14-ounce) can Eagle® Brand
Sweetened Condensed Milk
(NOT evaporated milk)
2 egg yolks*
½ cup ReaLemon® Lemon Juice
from Concentrate
1 teaspoon grated lemon rind,
optional
Yellow food coloring, optional

Preheat oven to 350°. Prepare and bake
cake mix as package directs for 13x9-inch
cake. Meanwhile, in medium bowl, beat
sweetened condensed milk and egg
yolks. Stir in ReaLemon® brand, rind and
food coloring if desired. Spread evenly
over hot cake. Return to oven; bake
8 minutes longer. Cool. Chill. Garnish as
desired. Refrigerate leftovers.

*Use only Grade A clean, uncracked eggs.

CHERRY DUMPLIN' CAKE　▲

(Makes 6 to 9 servings)

1 (21-ounce) can cherry pie filling
1 (14-ounce) can Eagle® Brand
Sweetened Condensed Milk
(NOT evaporated milk)
1 teaspoon almond extract
½ cup plus 2 tablespoons cold
margarine or butter
2½ cups biscuit baking mix
½ cup firmly packed brown sugar
½ cup chopped nuts

Preheat oven to 325°. In medium bowl,
combine pie filling, sweetened condensed
milk and extract. In large bowl, cut ½ cup
margarine into 2 cups biscuit mix until
crumbly. Stir in cherry mixture. Spread
in greased 12x7-inch baking dish. In
small bowl, combine remaining ½ cup
biscuit mix and sugar; cut in remaining
2 tablespoons margarine until crumbly.
Stir in nuts. Sprinkle evenly over cherry
mixture. Bake 1 hour to 1 hour and 10
minutes or until golden brown. Serve
warm with ice cream if desired.
Refrigerate leftovers.

MICROWAVE: In 2-quart round baking
dish, prepare as above. Cook on 100% power
(high) 16 to 18 minutes. Serve as above.

COCONUT LEMON TORTE

(Makes one 8- or 9-inch cake)

1 (14-ounce) can Eagle® Brand
   Sweetened Condensed Milk
   (NOT evaporated milk)
2 egg yolks
½ cup ReaLemon® Lemon Juice
   from Concentrate
1 teaspoon grated lemon rind,
   optional
   Yellow food coloring, optional
1 (18¼- or 18½-ounce) package
   white cake mix
1 (4-ounce) container frozen non-
   dairy whipped topping, thawed
   (1¾ cups)
   Flaked coconut

Preheat oven to 350°. In medium saucepan, combine sweetened condensed
milk, egg yolks, ReaLemon® brand, rind
and food coloring if desired. Over medium
heat, cook and stir until thickened, about
10 minutes. Chill. Meanwhile, prepare cake
mix as package directs. Pour batter into
two well-greased and floured 8- or 9-inch
round layer cake pans. Bake 30 minutes or
until lightly browned. Remove from pans;
cool thoroughly. With sharp knife, remove
crust from top of each cake layer. Split
layers. Spread equal portions of lemon
mixture between layers and on top to
within 1 inch of edge. Frost side and 1-inch
rim on top of cake with whipped topping.
Coat side of cake with coconut; garnish as
desired. Store covered in refrigerator.

BLUEBERRY & PEACH SHORTCAKE

(Makes 6 to 8 servings)

1 (8-ounce) package cream cheese,
   softened
1 (14-ounce) can Eagle® Brand
   Sweetened Condensed Milk
   (NOT evaporated milk)
⅓ cup plus 1 tablespoon ReaLemon®
   Lemon Juice from Concentrate
1 teaspoon vanilla extract
1 (6.5-ounce) prepared sponge
   cake layer
2 tablespoons sugar
2 teaspoons cornstarch
¼ cup water
1 cup fresh or frozen blueberries
   Sliced peaches

In large mixer bowl, beat cheese until
fluffy. Gradually beat in sweetened condensed milk until smooth. Stir in ⅓ cup
ReaLemon® brand and vanilla. Spread on
cake; chill. In small saucepan, mix sugar,
cornstarch, water and remaining 1 tablespoon ReaLemon® brand. Cook and
stir until thickened. Add blueberries;
cook until bubbly. Chill. Before serving,
top cake with peach slices and blueberry
sauce. Refrigerate leftovers.

Pictured opposite page from top: Coconut
Lemon Torte, Blueberry & Peach Shortcake.

CANDIES & CONFECTIONS

Pictured clockwise from top right:
Foolproof Dark Chocolate Fudge (recipe
page 102), Stained Glass Fudge (recipe
page 103), Triple Peanut Fudge, Chocolate
Truffles (recipes page 102), Milk Chocolate Fudge (variation of Foolproof Dark
Chocolate Fudge).

FOOLPROOF DARK CHOCOLATE FUDGE

(Makes about 2 pounds)

3 (6-ounce) packages semi-sweet chocolate chips (3 cups)
1 (14-ounce) can Eagle® Brand Sweetened Condensed Milk (NOT evaporated milk)
  Dash salt
½ to 1 cup chopped nuts
1½ teaspoons vanilla extract

In heavy saucepan, over low heat, melt chips with sweetened condensed milk and salt. Remove from heat; stir in nuts and vanilla. Spread evenly into wax paper-lined 8- or 9-inch square pan. Chill 2 hours or until firm. Turn fudge onto cutting board; peel off paper and cut into squares. Store loosely covered at room temperature.

MICROWAVE: In 1-quart glass measure, combine chips with sweetened condensed milk and salt. Cook on 100% power (high) 3 minutes or until chips melt, stirring after each 1½ minutes. Stir in remaining ingredients. Proceed as above.

Creamy Dark Chocolate Fudge: Melt 2 cups Campfire® Miniature Marshmallows with chips and sweetened condensed milk. Proceed as above.

Milk Chocolate Fudge: Omit 1 (6-ounce) package semi-sweet chocolate chips. Add 1 cup milk chocolate chips. Proceed as above.

Rocky Road Fudge: Omit 1 (6-ounce) package semi-sweet chocolate chips, salt, nuts and vanilla. In saucepan, melt chips with sweetened condensed milk and 2 tablespoons margarine or butter. In large bowl, combine 2 cups dry-roasted peanuts and 1 (10½-ounce) package Campfire® Miniature Marshmallows. Stir in chocolate mixture. Spread in wax paper-lined 13x9-inch pan. Proceed as above. (Makes about 2¾ pounds)

---

*CANDY COATING—also called confectioners' or summer coating is a general term used to describe chocolate-like products in which the cocoa butter has been replaced with vegetable fat. These flavored coatings are available where candy-making supplies are sold.

CHOCOLATE TRUFFLES

(Makes about 6 dozen)

3 (6-ounce) packages semi-sweet chocolate chips (3 cups)
1 (14-ounce) can Eagle® Brand Sweetened Condensed Milk (NOT evaporated milk)
1 tablespoon vanilla extract
  Finely chopped nuts, flaked coconut, chocolate sprinkles, colored sprinkles, unsweetened cocoa or colored sugar

In heavy saucepan, over low heat, melt chips with sweetened condensed milk. Remove from heat; stir in vanilla. Chill 2 hours or until firm. Shape into 1-inch balls; roll in any of the above coatings. Chill 1 hour or until firm. Store covered at room temperature.

MICROWAVE: In 1-quart glass measure, combine chips and sweetened condensed milk. Cook on 100% power (high) 3 minutes or until chips melt, stirring after each 1½ minutes. Proceed as above.

Tip: Omit vanilla. Add 3 tablespoons amaretto, orange-flavored liqueur, rum or bourbon if desired. Proceed as above.

TRIPLE PEANUT FUDGE

(Makes about 2 pounds)

1 (12-ounce) package peanut butter flavored chips
1 (14-ounce) can Eagle® Brand Sweetened Condensed Milk (NOT evaporated milk)
½ cup peanut butter
¾ cup chopped peanuts
1 teaspoon vanilla extract

In heavy saucepan, over low heat, melt chips with sweetened condensed milk and peanut butter. Remove from heat; stir in peanuts and vanilla. Spread evenly into wax paper-lined 8- or 9-inch square pan. Chill 2 hours or until firm. Turn fudge onto cutting board; peel off paper and cut into squares. Store loosely covered at room temperature.

MICROWAVE: In 1-quart glass measure, combine chips with sweetened condensed milk and peanut butter. Cook on 100% power (high) 3 minutes or until chips melt, stirring after each 1½ minutes. Proceed as above.

STAINED GLASS FUDGE

(Makes about 2¾ pounds)

- 1½ **pounds vanilla-flavored candy coating***
- 1 **(14-ounce) can Eagle® Brand Sweetened Condensed Milk (NOT evaporated milk)**
- ⅛ **teaspoon salt**
- 1½ **teaspoons vanilla extract**
- 1½ **cups chopped multi-colored gumdrops**

In heavy saucepan, over low heat, melt candy coating with sweetened condensed milk and salt. Remove from heat; stir in vanilla then gumdrops. Spread evenly into wax paper-lined 9-inch square pan. Chill 2 hours or until firm. Turn fudge onto cutting board; peel off paper and cut into squares. Store tightly covered at room temperature or in refrigerator.

MICROWAVE: In 2-quart glass measure, combine candy coating, sweetened condensed milk and salt. Cook on 100% power (high) 3 to 5 minutes or until melted, stirring after each 1½ minutes. Proceed as above.

Vanilla Nut Fudge: Omit multi-colored gumdrops. Add 1 cup chopped nuts. Proceed as above.

LAYERED MINT CHOCOLATE FUDGE

(Makes about 1¾ pounds)

- 1 **(12-ounce) package semi-sweet chocolate chips**
- 1 **(14-ounce) can Eagle® Brand Sweetened Condensed Milk (NOT evaporated milk)**
- 2 **teaspoons vanilla extract**
- 6 **ounces vanilla-flavored candy coating***
- 1 **tablespoon peppermint extract Green or red food coloring, optional**

In heavy saucepan, over low heat, melt chips with *1 cup* sweetened condensed milk; add vanilla. Spread *half* the mixture into wax paper-lined 8- or 9-inch square pan; chill 10 minutes or until firm. Hold remaining chocolate mixture at room temperature. In heavy saucepan, over low heat, melt candy coating with remaining sweetened condensed milk (mixture will be thick). Add peppermint extract and food coloring if desired. Spread on chilled chocolate layer; chill 10 minutes longer or until firm. Spread reserved chocolate mixture on mint layer. Chill 2 hours or until firm. Turn onto cutting board; peel off paper and cut into squares. Store loosely covered at room temperature.

*Also called confectioners' or summer coating—see page 102.

Layered Mint Chocolate Fudge

◀ TROPICAL CANDY CLUSTERS

(Makes about 5 dozen)

- 1 (11½-ounce) package milk chocolate chips
- 1 (6-ounce) package semi-sweet chocolate chips (1 cup)
- 1 (14-ounce) can Eagle® Brand Sweetened Condensed Milk (NOT evaporated milk)
- ¼ teaspoon salt
- 1½ cups coarsely chopped toasted almonds or macadamia nuts
- 1 cup chopped candied pineapple
- ½ to ¾ cup flaked coconut

In heavy saucepan, over low heat, melt chips with sweetened condensed milk and salt. Remove from heat; stir in remaining ingredients. Drop by heaping teaspoonfuls onto wax paper-lined baking sheets; chill 2 hours or until firm. Store covered in refrigerator.

MICROWAVE: In 2-quart glass measure, combine chips with sweetened condensed milk and salt. Cook on 100% power (high) 3 minutes or until chips melt, stirring after each 1½ minutes. Proceed as above.

◀ KENTUCKY BOURBON BALLS

(Makes about 15 dozen)

- 1½ cups finely chopped pecans
- ¼ cup bourbon
- ½ cup margarine or butter, softened
- 1 tablespoon vanilla extract
- 1 teaspoon salt
- 1 (14-ounce) can Eagle® Brand Sweetened Condensed Milk (NOT evaporated milk)
- 2 pounds plus 2 cups confectioners' sugar
- 1½ pounds chocolate-flavored candy coating*, melted

Soak pecans in bourbon 3 hours or overnight, stirring occasionally. In large mixer bowl, beat margarine, vanilla and salt until fluffy; gradually beat in sweetened condensed milk then pecan mixture and confectioners' sugar until well blended. Shape into 1-inch balls. Place on baking sheets. Chill until firm. With fork or wooden pick, dip each into warm candy coating; let excess coating drip off. Place on wax paper-lined baking sheets; let stand until firm. Store covered at room temperature or in refrigerator.

CREAMY ALMOND CANDY ▶

(Makes about 3¼ pounds)

- 1½ **pounds vanilla-flavored candy coating***
- 1 **(14-ounce) can Eagle® Brand Sweetened Condensed Milk (NOT evaporated milk)**
- ⅛ **teaspoon salt**
- 1 **teaspoon almond extract**
- 3 **cups whole almonds, toasted (about 1 pound)**

In heavy saucepan, over low heat, melt candy coating with sweetened condensed milk and salt. Remove from heat; stir in extract then almonds. Spread evenly into wax paper-lined 15x10-inch jellyroll pan. Chill 2 hours or until firm. Turn onto cutting board; peel off paper and cut into triangles or squares. Store tightly covered at room temperature.

MICROWAVE: In 2-quart glass measure, combine candy coating, sweetened condensed milk and salt. Cook on 100% power (high) 3 to 5 minutes, stirring after each 1½ minutes. Stir until smooth. Proceed as above.

CHOCO-PEANUT PINWHEELS ▶

(Makes about 1½ pounds)

- 1 **cup peanut butter flavored chips**
- 1 **(14-ounce) can Eagle® Brand Sweetened Condensed Milk (NOT evaporated milk)**
- 1 **(6-ounce) package semi-sweet chocolate chips (1 cup)**
- 1 **teaspoon vanilla extract**

Cut wax paper into a 15x10-inch rectangle; *butter paper*. In heavy saucepan, over low heat, melt peanut butter chips with ⅔ *cup* sweetened condensed milk. Cool slightly. With fingers, press evenly into thin layer to cover wax paper. Let stand at room temperature 15 minutes. In heavy saucepan, melt chocolate chips with remaining sweetened condensed milk. Remove from heat; stir in vanilla. Spread evenly over peanut butter layer. Let stand at room temperature 30 minutes. Beginning at 15-inch side, roll up tightly, jellyroll-fashion without wax paper. Wrap tightly in plastic wrap. Chill 2 hours or until firm. Cut into ¼-inch slices to serve. Store covered at room temperature.

*Also called confectioners' or candy coating—see page 102.

FONDANT EASTER EGGS ▲

(Makes 16 medium or 24 small eggs)

½ cup margarine or butter, softened
1 teaspoon salt
1 (14-ounce) can Eagle® Brand Sweetened Condensed Milk (NOT evaporated milk)
2 pounds plus 2 cups confectioners' sugar
Assorted food colorings
½ teaspoon vanilla, almond, lemon, maple or peppermint extract
1 pound chocolate- or vanilla-flavored candy coating*, melted
Decorator frosting

In large mixer bowl, beat margarine and salt until fluffy; gradually beat in sweetened condensed milk then 2 *pounds* confectioners' sugar until well blended. Divide into 4 equal portions. In medium bowl, tint *each* portion with few drops food coloring; flavor with ½ teaspoon desired extract. On surface, knead ¼ to ½ cup confectioners' sugar into each portion until smooth. Shape each portion into 4 or 6 eggs. Place on baking sheets; cover and chill until firm, about 4 hours or overnight. Insert 2-pronged fork into bottom of each chilled egg. Dip into warm candy coating; let excess coating drip off. Place on wax paper-lined baking sheets; let stand until firm. Decorate as desired with frosting. Store covered at room temperature or in refrigerator.

WHITE TRUFFLES ▲

(Makes about 8 dozen)

2 pounds vanilla-flavored candy coating*
1 (14-ounce) can Eagle® Brand Sweetened Condensed Milk (NOT evaporated milk)
1 tablespoon vanilla extract
1 pound chocolate-flavored candy coating*, melted, *or* unsweetened cocoa

In heavy saucepan, over low heat, melt vanilla candy coating with sweetened condensed milk. Remove from heat; stir in vanilla. Cool. Shape into 1-inch balls. With wooden pick, partially dip each ball into melted chocolate candy coating or roll in cocoa. Place on wax paper-lined baking sheets until firm. Store covered at room temperature or in refrigerator.

MICROWAVE: In 2-quart glass measure, combine vanilla candy coating and sweetened condensed milk. Cook on 100% power (high) 3 to 3½ minutes or until candy coating melts, stirring after each 1½ minutes. Proceed as above.

PEANUT BUTTER BLOCKS ▲

(Makes about 3 pounds)

1 (14-ounce) can Eagle® Brand
    Sweetened Condensed Milk
    (NOT evaporated milk)
1¼ cups creamy peanut butter
⅓ cup water
1 tablespoon vanilla extract
½ teaspoon salt
¼ cup cornstarch, sifted
1 pound vanilla-flavored candy
    coating*
2 cups Spanish peanuts,
    finely chopped

In heavy saucepan, combine sweetened condensed milk, peanut butter, water, vanilla and salt; stir in cornstarch. Over medium heat, cook and stir until thickened and smooth. Add candy coating; cook and stir until melted and smooth. Spread evenly into wax paper-lined 9-inch square pan. Chill 2 hours or until firm. Cut into squares; roll firmly in peanuts to coat. Store covered at room temperature or in refrigerator.

MICROWAVE: In 1-quart glass measure, combine sweetened condensed milk, peanut butter, water, vanilla and salt; stir in cornstarch. Cook on 100% power (high) 2 minutes; mix well. In 2-quart glass measure, melt candy coating on 50% power (medium) 3 to 5 minutes, stirring after each minute. Add peanut butter mixture; mix well. Proceed as above.

PEPPERMINT PATTIES ▲

(Makes about 8 dozen)

1 (14-ounce) can Eagle® Brand
    Sweetened Condensed Milk
    (NOT evaporated milk)
1 tablespoon peppermint extract
    Green or red food coloring, optional
6 cups confectioners' sugar
    Additional confectioners' sugar
1½ pounds chocolate-flavored candy
    coating*, melted

In large mixer bowl, combine sweetened condensed milk, extract and food coloring if desired. Add 6 cups sugar; beat on low speed until smooth and well blended. Turn mixture onto surface sprinkled with confectioners' sugar. Knead lightly to form smooth ball. Shape into 1-inch balls. Place 2 inches apart on wax paper-lined baking sheets. Flatten each ball into a 1½-inch patty. Let dry 1 hour or longer; turn over and let dry at least 1 hour. With fork, dip each patty into warm candy coating (draw fork lightly across rim of pan to remove excess coating). Invert onto wax paper-lined baking sheets; let stand until firm. Store covered at room temperature or in refrigerator.

*Also called confectioners' or summer coating—see page 102.

Pictured counterclockwise from left:
Hot Fudge Sauce (as fruit dip and ice
cream topping), Coconut Pecan Sauce,
Homemade Irish Cream Liqueur (recipes
page 110).

BEVERAGES, FROSTINGS & SAUCES

HOMEMADE IRISH CREAM LIQUEUR

(Makes about 5 cups)

1¼ to 1¾ cups Irish whiskey, brandy, rum, bourbon, scotch or rye whiskey
1 (14-ounce) can Eagle® Brand Sweetened Condensed Milk (NOT evaporated milk)
2 cups (1 pint) Borden® Whipping Cream or Coffee Cream
2 tablespoons chocolate-flavored syrup
2 teaspoons instant coffee
1 teaspoon vanilla extract
½ teaspoon almond extract

In blender container, combine ingredients; blend until smooth. Serve over ice. Store tightly covered in refrigerator. Stir before serving.

Homemade Cream Liqueurs: Omit Irish whiskey, chocolate-flavored syrup, coffee and extracts. Add 1¼ cups flavored liqueur (almond, coffee, orange or mint) to sweetened condensed milk and cream. Proceed as above.

Tip: For more blended flavor, store in refrigerator several hours before serving.

HOT FUDGE SAUCE

(Makes about 2 cups)

1 (6-ounce) package semi-sweet chocolate chips (1 cup), *or* 4 (1-ounce) squares semi-sweet chocolate
2 tablespoons margarine or butter
1 (14-ounce) can Eagle® Brand Sweetened Condensed Milk (NOT evaporated milk)
2 tablespoons water
1 teaspoon vanilla extract

In heavy saucepan, over medium heat, melt chips and margarine with sweetened condensed milk and water. Cook and stir constantly until thickened, about 5 minutes. Add vanilla. Serve warm over ice cream or as a fruit dipping sauce. Refrigerate leftovers.

MICROWAVE: In 1-quart glass measure, combine ingredients. Cook on 100% power (high) 3 to 3½ minutes, stirring after each minute. Proceed as above.

To Reheat: In small heavy saucepan, combine desired amount of sauce with small amount of water. Over low heat, stir constantly until heated through.

Spirited Hot Fudge Sauce: Add ⅓ cup almond, coffee, mint or orange-flavored liqueur after mixture has thickened.

COCONUT PECAN SAUCE

(Makes about 2 cups)

1 (14-ounce) can Eagle® Brand Sweetened Condensed Milk (NOT evaporated milk)
2 egg yolks, beaten
¼ cup margarine or butter
½ cup flaked coconut
½ cup chopped pecans
1 teaspoon vanilla extract

In heavy saucepan, combine sweetened condensed milk, egg yolks and margarine. Over medium heat, cook and stir until thickened and bubbly, about 8 minutes. Stir in remaining ingredients. Serve warm over ice cream or cake. Refrigerate leftovers.

MICROWAVE: In 1-quart glass measure, combine sweetened condensed milk, egg yolks and margarine. Cook on 70% power (medium-high) 4 to 5 minutes, stirring after 3 minutes. Proceed as above.

To Reheat: In small heavy saucepan, combine desired amount of sauce with small amount of water. Over low heat, stir constantly until heated through.

SPICY CARAMEL TOPPING

(Makes about 1¼ cups)

1 **(14-ounce) can Eagle® Brand Sweetened Condensed Milk (NOT evaporated milk), caramelized***
½ **teaspoon ground cinnamon**
¼ **teaspoon vanilla or almond extract**
Water

To Caramelize Eagle® Brand Sweetened Condensed Milk:
Oven Method: Pour 1 can sweetened condensed milk into 9-inch pie plate. Cover with aluminum foil; place in larger shallow pan. Fill larger pan with hot water. Bake at 425° for 1½ hours or until thick and caramel-colored. Beat until smooth.

Stovetop Method: Pour 1 can sweetened condensed milk into top of double boiler; place over boiling water. Over low heat, simmer 1 to 1½ hours or until thick and caramel-colored. Beat until smooth.

Microwave Method: Pour 1 can sweetened condensed milk into 2-quart glass measure. Cook on 50% power (medium) 4 minutes, stirring briskly every 2 minutes until smooth. Cook on 30% power (medium-low) 12 to 18 minutes or until very thick and caramel-colored, stirring briskly every 2 minutes until smooth.

Combine ingredients (add water to desired consistency); mix well. Serve warm over apple dumplings, ice cream, pound cake or with fresh fruit. Refrigerate leftovers.

To Reheat on Stovetop: In small heavy saucepan, combine desired amount of topping with small amount of water. Over low heat, stir constantly until heated through.

To Reheat in Microwave: Place desired amount of topping in a 1- or 2-cup glass measure. Heat on 100% power (high) 40 to 50 seconds or until warm, stirring after each 20 seconds.

Variations
Nutty Caramel Topping: Omit cinnamon. Increase vanilla to 1 teaspoon; add ⅓ cup chopped toasted nuts and 2 tablespoons flaked coconut.

Chocolate Caramel Topping: Omit cinnamon. Add 1 (1-ounce) square unsweetened chocolate, melted, to hot caramel topping; mix well. Increase vanilla to 1 teaspoon; add ⅓ cup chopped nuts if desired.

CREAMY HOT CHOCOLATE TODDY ▲

(Makes about 2 quarts)

1 (14-ounce) can Eagle® Brand Sweetened Condensed Milk (NOT evaporated milk)
½ cup unsweetened cocoa
1½ teaspoons vanilla extract
⅛ teaspoon salt
6 cups hot water
½ cup peppermint schnapps, white creme de menthe or Irish whiskey
Campfire® Marshmallows, optional

In large saucepan, combine sweetened condensed milk, cocoa, vanilla and salt; mix well. Over medium heat, gradually stir in water; heat through, stirring occasionally. Stir in schnapps. Top with marshmallows if desired. Refrigerate leftovers.

MICROWAVE: In 2-quart glass measure, combine all ingredients except schnapps and marshmallows. Heat on 100% power (high) 8 to 10 minutes, stirring every 3 minutes. Proceed as above.

HOLIDAY ORANGE NOG ▲

(Makes about 1½ quarts)

1 (14-ounce) can Eagle® Brand Sweetened Condensed Milk (NOT evaporated milk)
1 (6-ounce) can frozen orange juice concentrate, thawed
⅓ to ½ cup orange-flavored liqueur or brandy, optional
4 cups (1 quart) Borden® Half-and-Half
Yellow food coloring, optional
Orange slices
Ground cinnamon and nutmeg

In pitcher, combine sweetened condensed milk, juice concentrate and liqueur if desired; mix well. Just before serving, stir in half-and-half and food coloring if desired. Garnish with remaining ingredients. Refrigerate leftovers.

Tip: Recipe can be doubled.

LEMON CREAM CHEESE FROSTING ▲

(Makes about 2½ cups)

1 (14-ounce) can Eagle® Brand
   Sweetened Condensed Milk
   (NOT evaporated milk)
2 egg yolks
3 tablespoons ReaLemon® Lemon
   Juice from Concentrate
1 teaspoon vanilla extract
   Yellow food coloring, optional
1 (8-ounce) package cream cheese

In heavy saucepan, combine sweetened condensed milk, egg yolks and ReaLemon® brand. Over medium heat, cook and stir rapidly until thickened and bubbly, 4 to 5 minutes. Remove from heat; stir in vanilla and food coloring if desired. Chill thoroughly, about 1 hour. In small mixer bowl, beat cheese until fluffy. Gradually beat in lemon mixture until smooth. Use to frost one 8- or 9-inch two-layer, one 13x9-inch or 15x10-inch carrot, apple or spice cake. Refrigerate leftovers.

MAGIC-QUICK CHOCOLATE FROSTING ▲

(Makes about 1½ cups)

1 (14-ounce) can Eagle® Brand
   Sweetened Condensed Milk
   (NOT evaporated milk)
2 (1-ounce) squares semi-sweet or
   unsweetened chocolate
   Dash salt
3 tablespoons water
1 teaspoon vanilla extract

In heavy saucepan, combine sweetened condensed milk, chocolate and salt. Over medium heat, cook and stir rapidly until chocolate melts and mixture thickens, about 8 minutes. Remove from heat; stir in water and vanilla. Cook and stir rapidly until thickened again, about 4 minutes. Cool 10 minutes. Use to frost one 8- or 9-inch two-layer or one 13x9-inch cake or 2 dozen cupcakes. Store at room temperature.

FESTIVE CRANBERRY CREAM PUNCH

(Makes about 3 quarts)

Cranberry Ice Ring or ice
1 (14-ounce) can Eagle® Brand Sweetened Condensed Milk (NOT evaporated milk)
1 (12-ounce) can frozen cranberry juice cocktail concentrate, thawed
1 cup cranberry-flavored liqueur, optional
Red food coloring, optional
2 (1-liter) bottles club soda or ginger ale, chilled

Prepare ice ring in advance. In punch bowl, combine sweetened condensed milk, cranberry concentrate, liqueur and food coloring if desired. Just before serving, add club soda and Cranberry Ice Ring. Refrigerate leftovers.

Cranberry Ice Ring: Combine 2 cups cranberry juice cocktail with 1½ cups water. In 1½-quart ring mold, pour ½ cup cranberry liquid. Arrange ¾ to 1 cup cranberries and lime slices or mint leaves in mold; freeze. Add remaining 3 cups cranberry liquid to mold; freeze.

SPARKLING APPLE JACK CREAM

(Makes about 1¾ quarts)

1 (14-ounce) can Eagle® Brand Sweetened Condensed Milk (NOT evaporated milk)
1 cup apple-flavored liqueur
2 cups (1 pint) Borden® Whipping Cream, *unwhipped*
1 (750mL) bottle sparkling apple cider, chilled

In blender container, combine all ingredients except apple cider; blend until smooth. Just before serving, add apple cider; stir. Serve over ice. Garnish as desired. Refrigerate leftovers.

BLENDER CANDY BAR FROSTIES

(Makes about 1 quart)

1 (14-ounce) can Eagle® Brand Sweetened Condensed Milk (NOT evaporated milk)
1 (8-ounce) container Borden® Lite-line® Plain or Vanilla Yogurt
½ cup chocolate-flavored syrup
2 to 3 candy bars, broken
2 cups crushed ice

In blender container, combine ingredients; blend until smooth. Serve immediately. Garnish as desired. Refrigerate or freeze leftovers.

Double Chocolate Frosties: Omit candy bars; add 6 broken creme-filled chocolate sandwich cookies. Proceed as above. (Makes about 1 quart)

Fruit Frosties: Omit candy bars and chocolate-flavored syrup. Add 2 cups fresh strawberries, peaches or bananas. Proceed as above. (Makes about 1¼ quarts)

TROPICAL CREAM PUNCH

(Makes about 3 quarts)

1 (14-ounce) can Eagle® Brand Sweetened Condensed Milk (NOT evaporated milk)
1 (6-ounce) can frozen orange juice concentrate, thawed
1 (6-ounce) can frozen pineapple juice concentrate, thawed
2 (1-liter) bottles club soda, chilled

In punch bowl, combine sweetened condensed milk and juice concentrates; mix well. Add club soda; stir. Garnish as desired. Serve over ice. Refrigerate leftovers.

Pictured clockwise from top: Festive Cranberry Cream Punch, Sparkling Apple Jack Cream, Tropical Cream Punch, Blender Candy Bar Frostie.

HINTS FOR USING EAGLE BRAND

Eagle Brand is an all-natural concentrated blend of whole milk and sugar condensed by a special vacuum cooking process. It is entirely different from evaporated milk. Because it is a natural product, Eagle Brand may vary in color and consistency from can to can. Eagle Brand may also become thicker and more caramel-colored as its age or storage temperature increases. The performance of the product is not affected by these natural changes. The unopened product is safe and wholesome as long as the can seal is intact. If the sweetened condensed milk becomes unusually thick, stir briskly before using. If the product has become very caramelized, use in recipes where the caramel flavor is compatible with other ingredients such as peanut butter, butterscotch or chocolate.

REMOVAL FROM CAN

Remove entire end of can with can opener, then use rubber scraper to remove all of the sweetened condensed milk from the can.

EAGLE BRAND IS PRESWEETENED

Because Eagle Brand contains sugar which has already been thoroughly dissolved in the manufacturing process, most Eagle Brand recipes require no additional sugar.

STORAGE

Always store unopened cans of sweetened condensed milk in a cool, dry place. Do not store near range or other heat source.

MAGIC THICKENING

Because it is a precooked blend of milk and sugar, Eagle Brand thickens almost magically with the addition of acidic fruit juices like lemon juice or orange juice concentrate—to form delicious pie fillings, puddings and desserts *without cooking*.

Because it is a natural product, Eagle Brand may vary in color and consistency from can to can. These two photos illustrate the normal differences which may occur in Eagle Brand over time.

CARAMELIZATION

With the application of heat, sweetened condensed milk caramelizes, becoming thicker and more golden in color. In recipes such as Magic Cookie Bars, this process binds the ingredients together and produces a rich, caramel flavor. In addition, for many years, sweetened condensed milk has been heated by itself to make a caramel pudding or topping. For safety reasons, heating the *unopened* can (an old cooking method) is not recommended. To caramelize sweetened condensed milk, use one of the following methods.

TO CARAMELIZE EAGLE® BRAND SWEETENED CONDENSED MILK

Oven Method: Pour 1 can sweetened condensed milk into 9-inch pie plate. Cover with aluminum foil; place in larger shallow pan. Fill larger pan with hot water. Bake at 425° for 1½ hours or until thick and caramel-colored. Beat until smooth.

Stovetop Method: Pour 1 can sweetened condensed milk into top of double boiler; place over boiling water. Over low heat, simmer 1 to 1½ hours or until thick and caramel-colored. Beat until smooth.

Microwave Method: Pour 1 can sweetened condensed milk into 2-quart glass measure. Cook on 50% power (medium) 4 minutes, stirring briskly every 2 minutes until smooth. Cook on 30% power (medium-low) 12 to 18 minutes or until very thick and caramel-colored, stirring briskly every 2 minutes until smooth.

Serve caramelized sweetened condensed milk with fruit, chopped nuts, whipped cream or shaved chocolate.

CAUTION: NEVER HEAT UNOPENED CAN.

EAGLE BRAND & CHOCOLATE

When heated with chocolate, Eagle Brand quickly thickens to a velvety smooth consistency for candies and sauces that are never grainy or long-cooking. There's no need for constant stirring or a candy thermometer.

A NOTE ABOUT EGGS

Some recipes in this book specify, "Use only Grade A clean, uncracked eggs." This is a precaution given when uncooked or partially cooked eggs are called for, such as in recipes for egg nog, meringues, or pie fillings.

ICE CREAM MAKING

The thick creamy consistency of Eagle Brand helps to minimize the formation of ice crystals in ice creams and frozen desserts.

MICROWAVE

NOTE: Microwave ovens vary in wattage and power output; cooking times suggested in recipes may need to be adjusted. Check the cooking guide or instruction booklet for your microwave oven for specific information about the particular model you own. Always check for doneness at the minimum amount of time given in the recipe.

HINTS FOR DESSERT MAKING

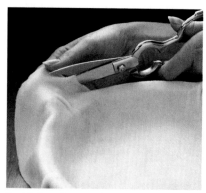

Use kitchen shears or sharp knife to trim dough ½ inch beyond pie plate edge. Fold under extra dough to form rim.

Flute edge as desired.

To keep an unfilled pastry crust from puffing or shrinking during baking, line with aluminum foil and fill with dry beans.

CRUMB CRUST

(Makes one 8- or 9-inch crust)

1½ cups graham cracker or chocolate
      wafer crumbs
¼ cup sugar
6 tablespoons margarine or
    butter, melted

Combine ingredients; mix well. Press firmly on bottom and up side to rim of 8- or 9-inch pie plate. Chill thoroughly or bake in preheated 375° oven 6 to 8 minutes or until edges are lightly browned. Cool before filling.

PASTRY CRUST

(Makes one 8- or 9-inch crust)

1 cup unsifted flour
½ teaspoon salt
⅓ cup shortening
3 to 4 tablespoons cold water

In medium bowl, combine flour and salt; cut in shortening until crumbly. Sprinkle with water, 1 tablespoon at a time, mixing until dough is just moist enough to hold together. Form dough into ball. Place on well-floured surface. Press down into a flat circle with smooth edges. Roll dough to a circle ⅛-inch thick and about 1½ inches larger than inverted pie plate. Ease dough into pie plate. Trim ½ inch beyond pie plate edge. Fold under; flute edge as desired.

◄ TO BAKE WITHOUT FILLING

Preheat oven to 450°. Prick bottom and side of pastry shell with fork. Line pastry with aluminum foil; fill with dry beans. Bake 5 minutes; remove beans and foil. Bake 5 to 7 minutes longer or until golden.

TO BAKE WITH FILLING

Preheat oven as directed in recipe. Do not prick pastry shell. Fill and bake as directed.

MICROWAVE TIPS

SOFTENING

Ingredient	Power Level	Time
½ cup margarine or butter	30% power (medium-low)	30 to 50 seconds
3 ounces cream cheese	50% power (medium)	30 to 60 seconds
8 ounces cream cheese	50% power (medium)	1 to 1½ minutes

MELTING

Ingredient	Power Level	Time
¼ cup margarine or butter	100% power (high)	45 to 60 seconds
½ cup margarine or butter	100% power (high)	45 seconds to 1½ minutes
1 cup margarine or butter	100% power (high)	1 to 2 minutes
1 cup chocolate chips	50% power (medium)	2½ to 3½ minutes
2 squares baking chocolate	50% power (medium)	2½ to 3½ minutes
4 squares baking chocolate	50% power (medium)	2½ to 4 minutes
4 ounces sweet cooking chocolate	50% power (medium)	2½ to 4 minutes
1 pound candy coating	50% power (medium)	3 to 5 minutes

CHOCOLATE LEAVES

Coat undersides of real leaves lightly with vegetable oil. Melt semi-sweet chocolate and coat undersides of leaves thickly with chocolate using small spoon or brush. Chill or freeze until firm, then peel away leaf.

WHIPPING CREAM

- Chill beaters and bowl thoroughly.
- Beat chilled whipping cream on high speed (overbeating or beating on low speed can cause cream to separate into fat and liquid).
- Beat only until stiff. Whipping cream doubles in volume.
- To sweeten whipped cream, gradually beat in 1 to 2 tablespoons granulated or confectioners' sugar and ½ to 1 teaspoon vanilla extract for each cup unwhipped whipping cream.

DISSOLVING GELATINE

To avoid lumpy gelatine mixtures, sprinkle unflavored gelatine over cold water; let stand 1 minute. Cook and stir over low heat until dissolved.

CHOCOLATE CURLS

With a vegetable parer or thin, sharp knife, slice across block of sweet milk chocolate or large-size milk chocolate candy bar with long, thin strokes. Chocolate should be at room temperature.

TOASTING COCONUT AND NUTS

Conventional Oven: Spread coconut or nuts in shallow pan. Toast in preheated 350° oven 7 to 15 minutes or until golden, stirring frequently.

Microwave Oven:

Coconut: Spread ½ cup coconut in glass pie plate. Cook on 70% power (medium-high) 5 to 10 minutes or until lightly browned, stirring after each minute.

Nuts: Spread 1 cup nuts in glass pie plate. Cook on 100% power (high) 5 to 8 minutes or until lightly browned, stirring after each minute.

NOTE: In a microwave oven, nuts heat quickly and brown evenly. Remove from oven as soon as they *begin* to brown (browning will continue as they stand). Pie plate and nuts will be very hot after toasting; handle carefully.

To split cake layer, measure halfway up side; mark with toothpicks. Using long piece of thread, rest on picks. Cross thread and pull through to split layers.

On humid or rainy days, substitute Foolproof Meringue for regular meringue to minimize weeping and shrinking.

FOOLPROOF MERINGUE

(For 9- or 10-inch pie)

½ cup sugar
1 tablespoon cornstarch
½ cup water
3 egg whites, at room temperature
   Dash salt

In small saucepan, combine 2 *tablespoons* sugar and cornstarch; stir in water until smooth. Over low heat, cook and stir until thickened. Cool. Meanwhile, in small mixer bowl, beat egg whites and salt to soft peaks. Gradually beat in cornstarch mixture until well blended. Gradually beat in remaining 6 *tablespoons* sugar until stiff peaks form. Spread on top of pie, sealing carefully to edge of shell. Bake in preheated 350° oven 25 minutes or until lightly browned. Cool. Chill.

For level layers, use a long thin serrated knife to slice off rounded or uneven top of cake.

To marble, gently swirl a narrow spatula through the light and dark mixtures.

GLOSSARY

DESSERT MAKING TERMS

Bake:
To cook by dry heat, usually in an oven.

Baking Dish:
Glass or ceramic container which can be used in oven.

Batter:
A mixture of ingredients that can be poured or dropped from a spoon.

Beat:
To mix by stirring rapidly in a circular motion by hand or with electric mixer.

Blend:
To mix two or more ingredients together until smooth or until they combine to produce a uniform texture, color or flavor.

Caramelize:
To cook sugar slowly until it melts and turns golden brown or to heat sweetened condensed milk until it becomes thick and caramel colored (see page 117).

Combine:
To mix two or more ingredients until blended.

Core:
To remove the center part of a fruit (apples, pears, etc.).

Cut In:
To mix solid fat into dry ingredients using a cutting motion (with pastry blender or two knives).

Drizzle:
To pour a liquid in a thin stream over a surface to create a pattern of irregularly spaced fine lines.

Fold:
To incorporate a light, aerated mixture into a heavier mixture with a lifting, circular motion, without deflating the lighter mixture.

Glaze:
To coat a surface with a thin layer of icing, chocolate, jelly, egg wash, etc., to give it a shiny finish.

Grate:
To grind solid food (lemon or orange rind, chocolate, coconut, etc.) against a grater to produce fine shreds, flakes or tiny particles.

Grease and Flour:
To spread a thin layer of solid shortening, butter, or oil on the inside of a baking pan and then coat the surface with a thin layer of flour.

Hull:
To remove the outer parts of nuts.
To remove stems and inner hard core from strawberries.

Knead:
To work dough with hands into a malleable mass by pressing and folding.

Line:
To cover the inside or just the bottom of a pan with a piece of aluminum foil, wax paper or parchment paper.

Pan:
Metal container to which direct heat can be applied (stove top, oven).

Pare/Peel:
To remove the rind or skin of a fruit.

Preheat:
To allow oven to heat to the desired temperature before placing food in oven (15 to 20 minutes).

Puree:
To blend, sieve or process into a soft, smooth consistency.

Simmer:
To cook just below the boiling point (180°F).

Stir:
To mix ingredients together with a spoon until well blended. Use a slow, wide, circular motion; do not beat.

Toast:
To toast nuts or coconut by baking in oven until light golden brown (or until nuts are crisp and dry).

Turn Out:
To remove a baked product from pan in which it was baked.

Whip:
To beat rapidly in a circular motion with a whisk or electric mixer in order to increase a mixture's volume by incorporating air into it.

INDEX

SIMPLY DELICIOUS DESSERTS

with Eagle® Brand
Sweetened Condensed Milk

- More than 150 New and Traditional Recipes, Each in Full Color
- Spiral Bound, Hardcover
- Convenient 5⅜'' x 8½'' size
- Money Saving Coupons Inside

SIMPLY DELICIOUS DESSERTS

with Eagle® Brand
Sweetened Condensed Milk

- More than 150 New and Traditional Recipes, Each in Full Color
- Spiral Bound, Hardcover
- Convenient 5⅜'' x 8½'' size
- Money Saving Coupons Inside

SIMPLY DELICIOUS DESSERTS

with Eagle® Brand
Sweetened Condensed Milk

- More than 150 New and Traditional Recipes, Each in Full Color
- Spiral Bound, Hardcover
- Convenient 5⅜'' x 8½'' size
- Money Saving Coupons Inside

MAIL-IN CERTIFICATE

To order your SIMPLY DELICIOUS DESSERTS Recipe Book, check the appropriate box below and send this completed form with:

☐ 1 Eagle® Brand label and $4.95 (check or money order) for each book ordered **OR**
☐ $6.95 (check or money order) with <u>NO</u> labels for each book ordered.

Enclosed is $_____ and _____ labels for _____ books.

Name_____

Address_____

City_____ State_____ Zip_____

Send completed form to: Simply Delicious Desserts
P.O. Box 9612-D, Clinton, Iowa 52736

BORDEN IF IT'S BORDEN-IT'S GOT TO BE GOOD

Offer good while supplies last. Void where restricted. This form required, no facsimiles accepted. Allow 8 weeks for delivery. Offer good only in U.S.A.
© Borden, Inc., 1991

MAIL-IN CERTIFICATE

To order your SIMPLY DELICIOUS DESSERTS Recipe Book, check the appropriate box below and send this completed form with:

☐ 1 Eagle® Brand label and $4.95 (check or money order) for each book ordered **OR**
☐ $6.95 (check or money order) with <u>NO</u> labels for each book ordered.

Enclosed is $_____ and _____ labels for _____ books.

Name_____

Address_____

City_____ State_____ Zip_____

Send completed form to: Simply Delicious Desserts
P.O. Box 9612-D, Clinton, Iowa 52736

BORDEN IF IT'S BORDEN-IT'S GOT TO BE GOOD

Offer good while supplies last. Void where restricted. This form required, no facsimiles accepted. Allow 8 weeks for delivery. Offer good only in U.S.A.
© Borden, Inc., 1991

MAIL-IN CERTIFICATE

To order your SIMPLY DELICIOUS DESSERTS Recipe Book, check the appropriate box below and send this completed form with:

☐ 1 Eagle® Brand label and $4.95 (check or money order) for each book ordered **OR**
☐ $6.95 (check or money order) with <u>NO</u> labels for each book ordered.

Enclosed is $_____ and _____ labels for _____ books.

Name_____

Address_____

City_____ State_____ Zip_____

Send completed form to: Simply Delicious Desserts
P.O. Box 9612-D, Clinton, Iowa 52736

BORDEN IF IT'S BORDEN-IT'S GOT TO BE GOOD

Offer good while supplies last. Void where restricted. This form required, no facsimiles accepted. Allow 8 weeks for delivery. Offer good only in U.S.A.
© Borden, Inc., 1991